awesome

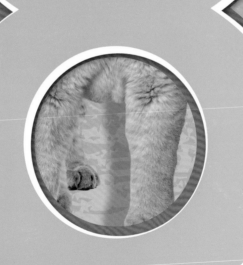

8

extreme

NATIONAL
GEOGRAPHIC
KIDS

awesome

8

eXtreme

SARAH WASSNER FLYNN
& BRITTANY MOYA DEL PINO

NATIONAL
GEOGRAPHIC
KiDS

WASHINGTON, D.C.

HEY THERE, AWESOME READERS!

ARE YOU READY ...

... to see some of the most amazing and extreme sights on our planet? Then you've come to the right book! There are so many places, people, and things to show you ... where to start? How about we just take it from the top:

WHAT IS *AWESOME 8 EXTREME*?

Awesome 8 eXtreme is a picture-packed list book of the coolest, craziest, and most extremely amazing things we could think of.

WHY EIGHT?

Well, why not? There are top ten lists—and if you ask us, eight is an extremely awesome number. Better than ten even, because that means the things on our list have to be even cooler to make the cut!

DO I HAVE TO START AT THE BEGINNING?

No way. This book was designed with you in mind. Pick up the book, flip to a page that interests you, and read away! Don't like a topic? Skip it. Love a topic? Read it twice!

WHAT ELSE IS IN THIS BOOK?

Awesome 8 eXtreme features superlative spreads showcasing everything from freaky frogs to forces of nature, from stunning shipwrecks to supersize sculptures. Along the way are fun facts and deeper dives where we take a closer look at some of the things and places featured.

ANYTHING ELSE I SHOULD KNOW?

Yes! There are some pretty awesome activities described in this book, but please don't try ANYTHING without first consulting an adult. Safety first, Awesome 8'ers. Now turn the page and jump on in!

TABLE OF CONTENTS

RAD REPLICAS

EVEN BETTER THAN THE REAL THING?
THESE RE-CREATIONS WILL MAKE YOU DO A DOUBLE TAKE.

2 ON POINT

A skilled sculptor carved these awesome **Darth Vaders** out of pencil points. He creates these and other cool copies by holding the pencil in one hand and a craft knife in the other.

THE SAME ARTIST ONCE CARVED A RACE CAR OUT OF A ONE-TON (0.9 mt) BLOCK OF CHEDDAR CHEESE.

1 THE BIG CHEESE

Say cheese! Cheddar, to be exact. A sculptor carved the likeness of the **U.S. Capitol** building out of a giant 400-pound (181-kg) block of the yellow cheese—enough to make some 50,000 sandwiches.

3 CAN-TASTIC

Talk about driving art to a whole new level! This cool **car** was a sculpture built out of canned food as part of an exhibition to raise awareness of hunger issues and collect donations for food banks.

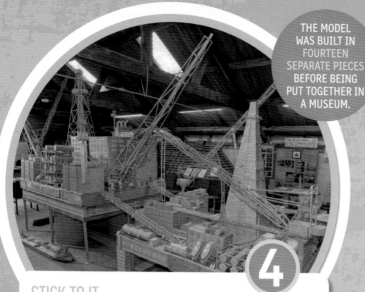

THE MODEL WAS BUILT IN FOURTEEN SEPARATE PIECES BEFORE BEING PUT TOGETHER IN A MUSEUM.

4 STICK TO IT

Four million matchsticks were used to create this copy of an **oil rig platform.** The artist spent some 30,000 hours over 15 years to piece together this half-ton (.45 mt) model of a rig similar to one he once worked on.

5 LITTLE LIBERTY

Lady Liberty doesn't just welcome visitors to the Big Apple: This famous green gal also raises her torch in front of the New York, New York hotel on the Las Vegas Strip. Except the copycat statue is just 150 feet (46 m) tall—half the height of the real deal.

7 IT'S ALL GREEK

It may be the exact same size and sport similar columns, but this building is far from the original **Parthenon** in Athens, Greece. This monument and museum at Centennial Park in Nashville, Tennessee, U.S.A., was built to mark the state's 100th anniversary in 1897.

6 BRIDGE IT

Think this is a pic of **London's Tower Bridge?** Think again! It's actually a smaller-scale reproduction of the iconic landmark, rising above a river in Suzhou, China. The structure is a centerpiece for this unique town, which features more than 50 other replica bridges.

8 BRICK BY BRICK

It took 120,000 Lego pieces to create this mini-version of London, England's **St. Pancras station.** Taller than a 10-year-old kid, the replica features 2,000 windows, four working clocks, and six working platforms allowing trains to scoot in and out.

Dressed-Up DOGS

THESE ARE SOME OF THE CUTEST CANINES IN COSTUME, PAWS DOWN!

2 TRÈS CUTE

It's only fitting that this adorable and **pint-size Pomeranian** is disguised as—what else?—pom frites, a play on the French phrase for french fries. Pass the ketchup!

1 BARK KENT

It's a bird, it's a plane, it's ... **super dog!** This playful pooch has the perfect costume for hitting Comic-Con—the world's largest comic-book event—in San Diego, California, U.S.A.

5

COUNTRY CANINE

Yee-haw! This **bulldog rocks the cowgirl** look, complete with a pink tutu, blonde braids peeking out from a black cowboy hat, and, of course, boots on each paw. All she needs is a horse. Giddyup!

8

ROCK AND ROLL OVER

He ain't nothing but a hound dog ... err, make that a shih tzu. This canine's disguised as the King of Rock—**Elvis Presley**—for a Halloween parade in New York City.

4

TALKING TURKEY

Dressed like a **Thanksgiving turkey**, this dog's so adorable you could almost eat him up! And he'd look even better with a side of mashed *paw*-tatoes. Woof!

7

POTTER PUP

Attention, Muggles (and *muttles*)! This **Hogwarts-bound pooch** channels the famous boy wizard by sporting his signature circular spectacles and wizardly cape. He must be on his way to *Gruffindor!*

3

THE DOG WHO CRIED WOLF

My, what big ears you have! While marching in the Haute Dog Howl'oween parade in Long Beach, California, U.S.A., this dog dresses up as **a wolf in Grandma's clothes** from the famous fairy tale *Little Red Riding Hood.*

DOUBLE TROUBLE

What's more adorable than a couple of **Minions?** A pair of pups dressed as Minions! These dogs are anything but despicable when dressed as the troublemaker cartoon characters for a puppy fashion show in the Philippines.

6

EIGHT Awe-Inspiring Sights in AFRICA

FROM THE SAVANNA TO THE CITIES, EXPLORE THESE EXTREMELY COOL SPOTS ON THE WORLD'S SECOND LARGEST CONTINENT.

①

JUST DUNE IT

Hop on a camel and explore the **Erg Chebbi,** giant hills of smooth sand rising up to 45 stories above the town of Merzouga in Morocco. Stretching into the Sahara, the deep orange and red dunes have served as a backdrop for several movies and TV shows.

(2)

ON THE TABLE

Towering 3,500 feet (1,000 m) over Cape Town, South Africa, **Table Mountain** is a top tourist spot in Africa. Visitors can zip up to its flat-topped peak on a cable car, where they'll find panoramic views of the city, island, and bay below.

MAJOR FALLS

Longer than 17 soccer fields and taller than a skyscraper, **Victoria Falls** on the Zambezi River is the world's largest sheet of falling water. During the rainy season, enough water spills over its sides every minute to fill some 200,000 swimming pools.

(5)

UP A TREE

Known as the "tree of life," the funky-looking **baobab** is a standout symbol of sub-Saharan Africa. The trees—whose trunk holds more than 1,000 gallons (4,000 L) of water—provide habitats for animals like snakes, bats, and bush babies.

(4)

(3)

GO APE

Trek through the misty peaks of Rwanda and you could land upon a wild **mountain gorilla**. Some 350 mountain gorillas—about half of those living around the world—can be found on the slopes of central Africa, including in the Rwandan rain forest.

(6)

THERE IS AN ACTIVE VOLCANO IN SERENGETI NATIONAL PARK THAT SPEWS WHITE LAVA.

FIRE ON THE MOUNTAIN

Rising two miles (3 km) over the Democratic Republic of the Congo, the **Nyiragongo volcano** is one of the most active on the planet. From its peak you can peer down into a bubbling lava lake, one of the world's largest.

(8)

(7)

WALK THIS WAY

Wind your way through and over the trees in the **Kirstenbosch National Botanical Garden** on this curved steel structure, nicknamed the "boomslang" after a type of extremely toxic tree snake! Follow it from the forest floor all the way up to the treetops for a spectacular view of surrounding Cape Town, South Africa.

WILD AND FREE

With a name meaning "endless plains" in the Maasai language, **Serengeti National Park** in Tanzania truly is a wildlife wonderland. Covering more than 5,700 square miles (14,763 sq km), this picturesque reserve is home to more than two million mammals, including lions, elephants, zebras, rhinos, and wildebeests.

TURN THE PAGE FOR MORE AMAZING AFRICA!

THE MYSTERY OF LAKE NATRON

HOW CAN THE AFRICAN LESSER FLAMINGO SURVIVE—AND THRIVE—IN SUCH HARSH WATERS?

AERIAL VIEW OF LESSER FLAMINGOS ON LAKE NATRON ▼

EIGHT OTHER UNUSUAL LAKES

1

WHAT: Jellyfish Lake, in Palau
WHY IT'S UNUSUAL: Jellyfish dominate this isolated saltwater lake in the South Pacific, which has an oxygen-less bottom layer that is life-threatening to people.

2

WHAT: Don Juan Pond, in Antarctica
WHY IT'S UNUSUAL: The saltiest water on Earth, this lake never freezes despite its frigid environment.

3

WHAT: Lake Nong Harn, in Thailand
WHY IT'S UNUSUAL: Each fall, hundreds of thousands of bright red lotus flowers completely cover this 8,000-acre (3,237-ha) lake.

4

WHAT: Boiling Lake, in Dominica
WHY IT'S UNUSUAL: Temps of this superhot lake top 180°F (82°C), and its center stays at a constant rolling boil.

It's oozing with slimy algae and invisible—but deadly—bacteria. It's so toxic that most animals attempting to swim in its burning hot waters quickly perish, their skeletons eventually littering the barren landscape. This is Africa's Lake Natron, notorious for its ultra-hostile environment and one of the least hospitable places on the planet. Situated on the border of Tanzania and Kenya, Lake Natron has rust-colored water (the result of a mix of salt and algae) and harmful fumes that can kill a human after a prolonged exposure. Yet, mysteriously, one type of bird not only survives in Lake Natron—it thrives there, too. Every

fall, African lesser flamingos flock to the lake's banks to breed, producing hundreds of thousands of hatchlings. So how are these birds able to survive such extreme conditions?

It actually has a lot to do with the time of the year that the flamingos visit Lake Natron, as well as the location of their nests. Because they land on the lake in the fall and winter when the water levels are low, there's simply less water to worry about. Another helpful factor: The birds build their nests on the cone-shaped mud mounds that form around the lake, keeping their eggs—and eventually their chicks—protected from flooding and from

predators like hyenas. And because the flamingo's dietary staples are the blue-green algae and larvae that thrive in super-salty lakes like Natron, there's plenty of food to keep the whole flock healthy. So unless they accidentally fall into the deadly water, the birds mostly stay safe.

Actually, the biggest threat to lesser flamingos isn't Lake Natron's toxic conditions. It's humans who want to mine the ash around the lake, which experts say would cause a dangerous disruption to the breeding habits of these birds. Currently, conservationists are working to squelch these plans—and save the future of the flamingos.

NESTING COLONY OF LESSER FLAMINGOS, LAKE NATRON, TANZANIA

5
WHAT: Lake Baikal, in Russia
WHY IT'S UNUSUAL: The world's deepest and most voluminous lake, Baikal holds some 20 percent of Earth's freshwater supply.

6
WHAT: Lake Nyos, in Cameroon
WHY IT'S UNUSUAL: Deep thermal pockets of methane gas cause killer explosions at the surface of this lake.

7
WHAT: Medicine Lake, in Canada
WHY IT'S UNUSUAL: Like a giant bathtub being emptied, the water completely drains from the bottom of this glacial lake every winter.

8
WHAT: Lake Balkhash, in Kazakhstan
WHY IT'S UNUSUAL: A narrow strait divides this lake into two parts: One is freshwater and one is brackish, or a mix of salt and freshwater.

13

EIGHT PIECES OF AMAZING ART

SET YOUR SIGHTS ON THESE MIND-BOGGLING MASTERPIECES AND WEIRD WORKS OF ART.

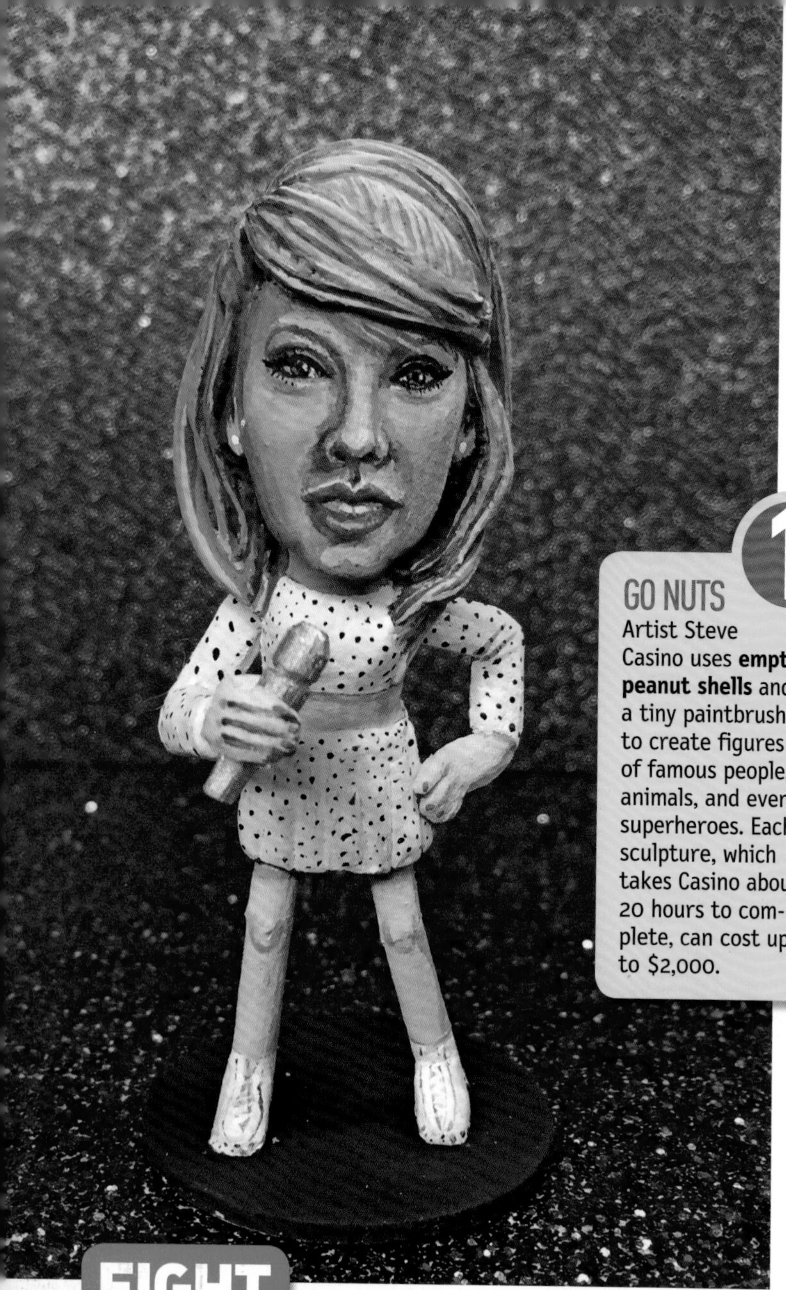

1 GO NUTS

Artist Steve Casino uses **empty peanut shells** and a tiny paintbrush to create figures of famous people, animals, and even superheroes. Each sculpture, which takes Casino about 20 hours to complete, can cost up to $2,000.

TEA HAS BEEN AROUND FOR THOUSANDS OF YEARS, BUT TEA BAGS WERE INVENTED ONLY A CENTURY AGO.

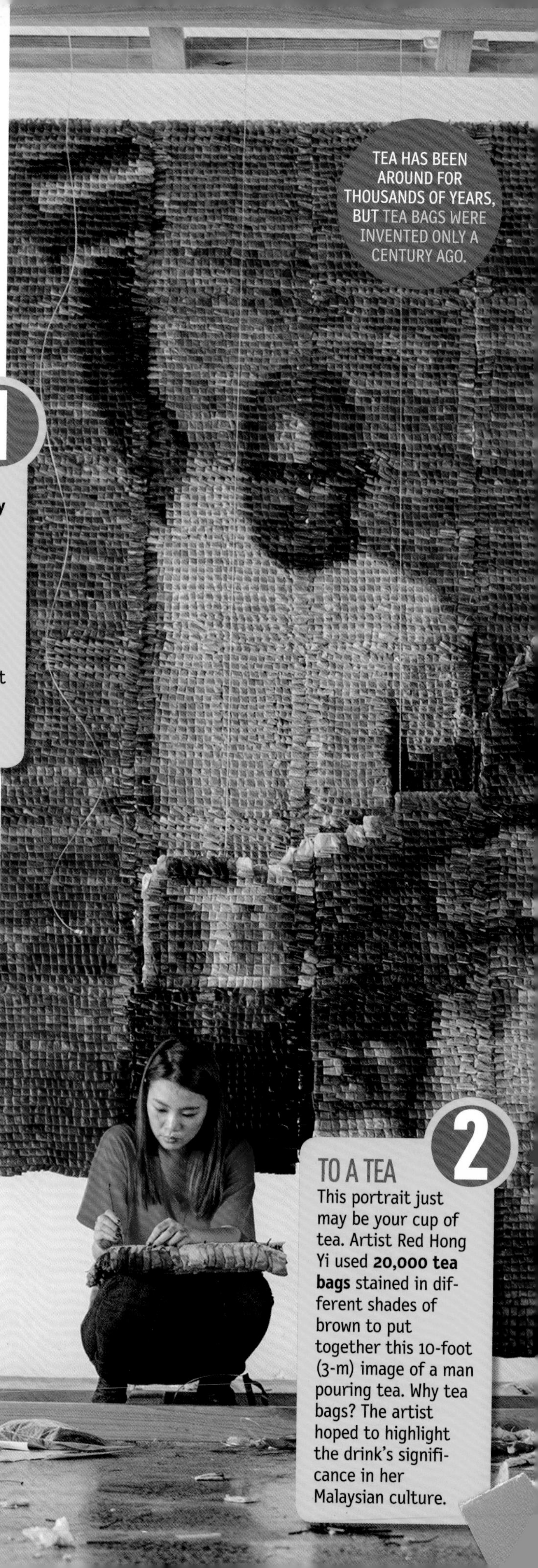

2 TO A TEA

This portrait just may be your cup of tea. Artist Red Hong Yi used **20,000 tea bags** stained in different shades of brown to put together this 10-foot (3-m) image of a man pouring tea. Why tea bags? The artist hoped to highlight the drink's significance in her Malaysian culture.

JERKYING AROUND

Artist Jason Mecier turns bits of beef jerky into **incredibly lifelike mosaics** like this Sasquatch. Each portrait takes some 50 bags of the dried meat and 50 hours to finish—and that doesn't include time for snacking.

4

3

WASTE NOT

This **junk sculpture** is for the birds! For Michelle Reader—who scours junkyards and thrift shops for materials for her masterpieces—one person's trash is an artist's treasure. Toys, clocks, and coffee cups have all been repurposed into her stunning sculptures.

5

NAILED IT

British artist Kayleigh O'Connor uses a steady hand—and plenty of creativity—to create **tiny 3-D images** on each of her (fake) fingernails.

MISSING SOMETHING?

These **bronze sculptures** may look like an optical illusion, but they were purposely created to appear as though they're missing most of their middle. Why? French artist Bruno Catalano says it's a statement on travelers who leave parts of themselves behind when they venture somewhere new.

7

6

PERFECT PIE

This **Santa** looks downright delicious! Domenico Crolla, pizza-making master and owner of the restaurant Bella Napoli, in Glasgow, Scotland, has created culinary portraits of celebrities including queens, supermodels, and musicians using mozzarella cheese and tomato sauce on a dough canvas. Yum!

8

SO SICK

This sculpture may not be feeling so well. Abstract artist Klaus Weber carved this **misshapen human figure** out of dark rock. With water continuously spewing from its mouth, it's no surprise that this work is often called the "Puking Fountain."

WACKY INVENTIONS

WHY DIDN'T WE THINK OF THAT?! HERE ARE SOME OF THE MOST EXTREMELY INNOVATIVE THINGS PEOPLE HAVE COME UP WITH.

1 MOP IT UP

Sometimes, mopping the floor can make you want to break out into song. If you have a **Mop Star,** you can sing while you clean, thanks to a built-in microphone on the handle of the mop.

2 SAY CHEESE

Because it's just so darn hard to take a good pic of your pup, enter the **Pooch Selfie:** a clip-on accessory that's meant to draw your dog's attention to your phone. Just show your pet this bright-colored, squeaky squeeze ball and you can get that shot in a snap.

3 GO FISH

Give your goldfish a view beyond the four walls of your room by popping him in this **mobile aquarium.** This rolling platform is set on sturdy wheels—meaning your fish won't go flying if you hit a bump in the road.

4 EAT AND RUN

To promote eating tomatoes on the, uh, run, a Japanese inventor came up with this **wearable robot.** If you're sporting this kooky contraption, just press a button and you'll have a juicy ripe tomato in your mouth in seconds.

WHY TOMATOES? SOME THINK THE RED FRUIT CAN FIGHT OFF FATIGUE WHILE YOU RUN.

5 FACE TIME

Picture this: You reach for a piece of toast from the toaster and up pops a slice with your face burned into the bread! That's what you get with the **Selfie Toaster,** a wacky gadget that uses a stainless-steel stencil of your mug to brand your bread.

6 SNORE NO MORE

Here's a bear-y interesting way to get you to stop snoring: When you start sawing logs, this **bear-shaped pillow** gently nudges your face with its paw! A sensor triggers the robot's light touch, nudging the sleeper to switch positions and putting a stop to the snoring.

7 SLICE AND BITE

Talk about multitasking! With this **handy gadget,** you can slice pizza and then eat it right up with a fork. The two-in-one utensil *seems* like a great idea, but you better watch out for that sharp blade when you dig in to your slice. Ouch!

8 SQUEEZE PLAY

You can't help but "like" this **ingenious inflatable jacket.** When you slip it on and update your Facebook status, it'll inflate and "hug" you every time one of your friends likes your post. Want to return the love? Simply deflate the jacket to send a "like" back to your buds.

DESERT OASIS

1

Nestled within the shadows of giant sand dunes is the village of Huacachina, Peru. Despite being in one of the planet's driest climates, this **tucked-away town** is an oasis of green, with palm trees and a peaceful lake believed to have healing powers.

EIGHT
HIDDEN PLACES REVEALED

STEP INTO SECRET SPOTS THAT ARE OFF-THE-CHARTS INCREDIBLE.

CAVED IN

2

Carved into a rocky overhang in the countryside of Sri Lanka is this network of five amazingly preserved temples. The **Dambulla Cave temples** feature an array of artifacts, from Buddha statues to colorful cave murals—all miraculously maintained, despite being thousands of years old.

4 UNBURIED TREASURE

A team of cavers spent several hours navigating a deep, **stalactite-covered cave** in Israel before they happened upon a treasure trove of ancient coins. Believed to have been buried for 2,300 years, the rare coins featured images of Alexander the Great and the god Zeus.

3 PARADISE FOUND

To get to the secreted-away Sekumpul Falls, you have to trek for about three hours into the lush, emerald green jungles of Bali, an island in Indonesia. But the hike is worth it to watch these **spectacular falls** flowing off a cliff that's nearly as tall as the Statue of Liberty.

DISNEY IN DISGUISE 5

Look closely at the fire station on Disneyland's Main Street, U.S.A. and you just may spot a second-floor balcony leading to Walt Disney's **secret apartment.** The man behind the mouse had the place built so he wouldn't miss any of the magic at the popular park.

6 BEHIND THE BOOKS

The Nebraska State Library is full of books—and a few tiny nooks that you can access only through **secret doors.** Some of the library's bookcases roll out to reveal doors that lead to hallways or small outdoor balconies.

WHAT LIES BENEATH 7

What used to be a busy network of trolley tunnels beneath the streets of Washington, D.C., has been transformed into **Dupont Underground,** an event space and gallery. Descend a staircase from the sidewalk and you can check out impressive exhibits that bring new meaning to underground art.

8 FALL FOR IT

Legend has it that Secret Caverns, **a network of caves** in upstate New York, was discovered when a cow accidentally fell into a deep hole. When the animal's owner went to rescue it, he discovered a 100-foot (30-m) waterfall. Today, you can tour this landmark, including those hidden falls.

WHEN IT COMES TO THE FUN FACTOR, THESE PLAYTHINGS ARE GAME-CHANGERS.

IT TOOK ONE WOMAN MORE THAN SIX MONTHS TO COMPLETE THIS GIANT PUZZLE.

2 TUB TIME
Here's one way to liven up a party! Seafarers in Seattle, Washington, U.S.A., can rent electric boats with a **built-in hot tub,** offering a double dose of relaxation and fun.

1 PIECE BY PIECE
Here's something that could really boost your bonding time with your family: a **32,000-piece jigsaw puzzle!** In the box, the pieces weigh a whopping 42 pounds (19 kg). And once complete? The puzzle takes up more floor space than you'll find in most living rooms.

3 VIRTUAL REALITY
The force is strong with this **arcade game,** where you can step inside a pod to reenact some of your favorite *Star Wars* scenes and battles. Bursts of air and vibrations make you feel like you really are in a galaxy far, far away.

BOUNCE BACK

You don't have to apologize when you bump into someone in this bizarre bubble. Whether you're playing soccer or just running around in circles, bouncing off one another is all part of the game with these **inflatable plastic orbs.**

5

GOLDEN GAME

It takes more than Monopoly money to get your hands on this **blinged-out version of the classic board game,** which features 18-karat-gold details and gemstones adding glitz to each property box. Even the pair of dice is bedazzled, with 42 diamonds standing in for the dots.

6

CHILD'S PLAY

Some lucky kids make themselves right at home in **mini-mansions**—elaborate playhouses that can cost tens of thousands of dollars. Many of these fancy abodes feature working electricity, heat, air-conditioning, and running water.

7

SUPER FALL

Superman has always been able to leap tall buildings in a single bound. And now he can **travel high above Earth**—or at least a plastic figurine of the superhero can. A team of tinkerers launched the toy into the stratosphere on a special balloon, attaching a camera to catch its free fall from 24 miles (39 km) up.

8

SLIP AND SLIDE

Who needs a water park when you can unfurl this **mega slide** in your backyard? Simply hook up your hose to this 25-foot (7.6-m) chute, take a running start, and see how far you can get. An ultra-slick surface means you'll fly even faster.

Furious FORCES

WHEN MOTHER NATURE SHOWS HER TEMPER, WATCH OUT!

STORMS NORTH OF THE EQUATOR SPIN COUNTERCLOCK- WISE; THOSE BELOW THE EQUATOR SPIN CLOCKWISE.

VIOLENT VORTEX

Tornadoes hold the title for most violent type of storm because of their intensity. Born from supercell thunderstorms, with wind speeds topping 200 miles an hour (321 km/h), they have enough power to squash buildings, uproot trees, and park cars on roofs.

SPACE WALLOP

Did you know that the sun has weather, too? Those giant erupting bubbles of magnetic gas are **solar storms.** Mega flares even have the ability to knock out our power and radio transmissions!

FIRESTORM!

Clouds boom with thunder, a volcano belches fire and brimstone, the sky rains ash while purple lightning bolts slash up from the ground. This is what meteorologists call a **dirty thunderstorm.** They don't understand why it happens, but it looks really cool.

RADICAL RIFTS

An earthquake's violent shake reminds us that major continental plates on the surface of our planet roll like conveyor belts—up at one end, down at the other—in what geologists call **plate tectonics.** These landmasses get stuck at the edge, or fault, and build up stored energy like a loaded spring until it's time to rumble!

SENSATIONAL SWIRL

Imagine all electricity produced around the world. Now take half of that energy—about 1.5 trillion watts—and bottle it in a swirling cloud 825 miles (1,327 km) across, one that dumps enough rain to fill 22 million Olympic-size pools. You've just made a **hurricane!**

MIGHTY MAELSTROMS

Stay away from that big swirly thing! That's a **maelstrom,** or "grinding stream" in translation from the Dutch. Fast-flowing waters can produce turbulent whirlpools with enough power to whip a boat around.

GLACIAL MELTDOWN

With a thunderous roar and crack, warming **glaciers** lose huge chunks of ice near their edges. As the resulting icebergs tumble into the ocean, they can spawn waves as tall as a house. Surf's up, dudes!

SHOCKING SPLASH

Rogue waves form during storms when multiple wave sets combine or when strong winds squish wave sets together, creating a solitary wall of water that could swallow a six-story building.

TURN THE PAGE FOR MORE EARTH-SHATTERING INFO!

SMOLDERING CORE

WHAT'S HAPPENING BENEATH OUR PLANET'S SURFACE?

Earth may have some wacky weather, but our planet's fiercest forces don't even scratch the surface. They're actually in the core, 1,800 miles (2,900 km) beneath our feet. At this depth, molten metal and rock roasts about as hot as the surface of the sun, and the pressure approaches what you'd feel if 132 blue whales (the largest animal on Earth) were balanced on your thumb! Despite famous books that romanticize what it would be like to go to the center of our world, no living thing could actually survive there. But, as it turns out, nothing could survive up here on the surface, either, without the power of our planet's core.

Earth gets warmer the deeper you go toward its center. Some of this heat, scientists believe, is left over from the big bang, an epic blast that scattered energy-charged matter and created our universe more than 13 billion years ago. Some of the heat also comes from the radioactive decay of elements like potassium, thorium, and uranium deep in the belly of our planet.

Beneath the crust and mantle, Earth's core actually has two layers: the outer core, which resembles a great, spherical swimming pool of nuclear-hot liquid metal (mostly iron and nickel, with sulfur and precious metals mixed in), and the inner core, where pressure is so intense that liquid metal is forced into a huge, rotating crystal that's superdense and about twice as wide as the state of Texas. This giant disco ball may not be as toasty as the liquid core above it, but it's still scorching hot: about 9392°F (5200°C).

Scientists can't send equipment to the core to take measurements, so they make guesses about what's happening below by studying earthquake vibra-tions, satellite pictures, and ancient rocks belched out of volcanoes. These methods suggest that our planet's core acts like an enormous dynamo, or engine. Hot metal in the liquid outer core expands and rises, losing heat as it travels toward the surface, and then sinking toward the center after it has cooled. This swirling motion creates a humongous planet magnet!

What's so great about a planet magnet? Here on the surface of Earth, it's good for migrating animals and for the Global Positioning Systems on our phones. But far more important, the planet's magnetic field is what shields us from the pulsing radioactive particle blasts given off by our sun—blasts that would kill every living thing if they hit us full force. So, thank your lucky stars for that furious fire and brimstone down under. Because without it, we'd all be toast!

DETERMINED TO DIG INTO THE EARTH? HERE ARE EIGHT DEEPLY COOL THINGS YOU MIGHT PASS ALONG THE WAY...

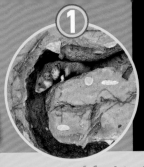

1

Within the first **6 feet** (2 m): small mammal burrows

2

Down to **10 feet** (3 m): earthworms and most plant roots

3

Down to **12 feet** (3.6 m): lizard burrows

4

At **400 feet** (122 m): the deepest known tree roots

5

At **2.4 miles** (3.9 km): the deepest point humans have ever reached underground, inside the TauTona gold mines of South Africa

6

At **6.8 miles** (11 km): the deepest point of any ocean, the floor of the Mariana Trench, in the Pacific Ocean

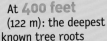

7

Between **15 and 37 miles** (25 and 60 km): the Mohorovicic Discontinuity (aka, the Moho), the boundary separating Earth's crust from its mantle

8

Beyond **93 miles** (150 km): the zone where diamonds form

EIGHT THRILLING THEATERS

FORGET THE FILM: SIMPLY SITTING IN THESE SEATS IS PURE ENTERTAINMENT. PASS THE POPCORN!

IN RUINS

Once the site of gladiator fights, this **ancient Roman amphitheater** in Pula, Croatia, could hold more than 20,000 spectators. Today the site hosts an annual film festival, where you can catch a movie inside these remarkable ruins.

2

SUN PICTURES IS THE WORLD'S OLDEST OPEN-AIR CINEMA.

SHARK BAIT

At the **Texas Ski Ranch** in New Braunfels, Texas, U.S.A., brave moviegoers watch the classic film *Jaws* while floating in rafts on a murky, man-made lake. Let's hope for their sake life doesn't imitate art ...

1

VINTAGE VIEWING

Talk about a throwback! **Sun Pictures** in Australia's outback has been in business since 1916, when the open-air theater showed silent films. Today you can grab a seat in a deck chair and catch the latest blockbusters.

3

HOT TUB PARTY

You can really *soak* it all in at the **Hot Tub Cinema** in London, England, where guests lounge in hot tubs instead of standard seats. Singing and dancing are encouraged, making this more of a party than a serious screening.

COOL AND COMFY

4

Located in the Notting Hill area of London, England, the **Electric Cinema Portobello** offers viewers some super-luxurious seating options: 65 leather armchairs with footstools, a few sofas in the back, and six double beds—yes, beds!—in the front row.

GRAVEYARD WATCH

6

Watching a film in a cemetery may sound like the stuff of horror movies, but at the **Cinespia** in Hollywood, California, U.S.A., there's nothing to be scared about. Groups of movie-goers spread out on the graveyard's grassy fields, catching a film under the stars.

THEATER WITH A VIEW

7

With a view like this, who needs a movie? At the **Rooftop Cinema** in Melbourne, Australia, films are shown from some six stories up. Surrounded by an epic skyline, you'll take in a movie *and* the sights.

SUN BEAM

8

Known as the world's smallest movie theater, the **Sol Cinema** seats just eight people. Housed in a tiny trailer, the theater travels throughout the United Kingdom, beaming films to the screen with renewable energy harnessed from the sun through solar panels.

GOING FOR GOLDS

1

THE GAMES: Rio de Janeiro, Brazil, 2016
THE EPIC DETAILS: Swimmer **Michael Phelps** made a giant splash in the sports world by winning eight events in the 2008 games—the most gold medals earned in a single Olympics. With his success in Rio, he has amassed an astounding 28 medals to date. He is the most decorated Olympian of all time.

EIGHT
EPIC **OLYMPIC** MOMENTS

FASTER, HIGHER, STRONGER! CHECK OUT PERFORMANCES FROM THE SUMMER AND THESE GOLDEN WINTER GAMES.

FLIPPING OUT

2

THE GAMES: London, England, 2012
THE EPIC DETAILS: American athlete **Gabby Douglas** leaped her way into the history books by becoming the first African-American gymnast to grab gold in the all-around event. She also helped Team U.S.A. score back-to-back team golds in 2012 and 2016.

DOUBLE TIME

THE GAMES: Atlanta, Georgia, U.S.A., 1996

THE EPIC DETAILS: In a duo of world-record performances, American sprinter **Michael Johnson** blew away the competition in the 200-meter and 400-meter events on the track—the first man to win both events in a single Olympics.

4

EXTREME AIR

THE GAMES: Sochi, Russia, 2014

THE EPIC DETAILS: Skiers showed off their high-flying moves for the first time on an Olympic stage in the **ski half-pipe**, which debuted in Sochi. In this event, athletes catch major air by shooting up and down a steep, two-sided ramp.

3

COLD CALL

THE GAMES: Calgary, Canada, 1988

THE EPIC DETAILS: It never snows on the island of Jamaica, but that didn't stop a four-man **bobsled crew** from racing in the '88 games—the first ever team from the country to compete in the Winter Olympics.

5

CROWD PLEASER

THE GAMES: London, England, 2012

THE EPIC DETAILS: Brit **Mo Farah** shocked everyone—even himself!—by winning the men's 5,000-meter race in front of a supportive crowd of countrymen. Having grown up not too far from the site of London's Olympic Stadium, Farah is now the United Kingdom's most decorated distance runner.

7

JUMP UP

THE GAMES: London, England, 2012

THE EPIC DETAILS: American **Richard Browne**, a below-the-knee amputee, soared in the men's high jump in the London Paralympics. Each year, athletes with a range of physical disabilities go for the gold in more than 20 sports, including track and field.

6

DREAM GAME

THE GAMES: Lake Placid, New York, U.S.A., 1980

THE EPIC DETAILS: When a hockey team made up of American college kids beat professional players from the Soviet Union 4–3, the **"Miracle on Ice"** went down as one of the greatest upsets in sports history.

8

EIGHT Spooky GHOST Towns

PEEK INTO THE HAUNTING STORIES BEHIND FORGOTTEN AND ABANDONED PLACES AROUND THE WORLD.

WHERE: UFO Houses, Sanzhi, Taiwan
WHY IT'S SPOOKY: These **UFO-shaped condos** once served as vacation homes for wealthy locals and U.S. military officers deployed in the area. Legend says that the pods, built on a graveyard, were cursed—and eventually business busted, leaving only shells of the odd buildings behind.

①

2

WHERE: Apice, Italy

WHY IT'S SPOOKY: A duo of powerful earthquakes shook **Apice** in the early 1960s, and the town has been all but abandoned ever since. Only a few residents remained, including the town's barber—who somehow stayed in business until 2012.

YOU CAN EXPLORE HASHIMA ISLAND FROM HOME VIA GOOGLE STREET VIEW.

3

WHERE: Bodie, California, U.S.A.

WHY IT'S SPOOKY: During the California Gold Rush, **Bodie** bustled with some 10,000 residents, plus restaurants, hotels, a bank, and even a bowling alley. As people began seeking gold elsewhere, they left Bodie behind, where it remains crumbling and covered in dust.

4

WHERE: Hashima Island, Japan

WHY IT'S SPOOKY: Once a spot for mining coal beneath the sea, **Hashima Island** was considered the most densely populated place on Earth in the late 1950s. When business slowed, its inhabitants left; today, the isolated island is empty.

5

WHERE: Route 66, U.S.A.

WHY IT'S SPOOKY: A highway linking Chicago to Los Angeles, **Route 66** was once a popular passage for people heading west. Traffic slowed when the road was decommissioned as a federal highway in 1985, leaving many towns' motels, gas stations, and roadside attractions boarded up.

6

WHERE: Varosha Resort, Cyprus

WHY IT'S SPOOKY: In 1974, a military invasion forced residents to flee this **once luxe resort,** and the area was ultimately fenced off for good. Those who have ventured inside report eerie scenes like a car showroom still stocked with decades-old cars.

8

WHERE: Chernobyl, Russia

WHY IT'S SPOOKY: An **epic nuclear blast** at a power plant decimated this town more than 25 years ago, forcing some tens of thousands of residents to leave with little notice. Today, classrooms, homes, and shops remain frozen in time.

7

WHERE: St. Elmo, Colorado, U.S.A.

WHY IT'S SPOOKY: For a mining town that emptied out about a century ago, **St. Elmo** is in surprisingly good condition. Most of the original houses and buildings are still standing, and you can even spend the night in a cabin there—if you dare.

TURN THE PAGE TO VISIT MORE UNUSUAL TOWNS!

WHEN THE
BOOM
WENT
BUST

EIGHT SUPER-SMALL AMERICAN TOWNS

THE PLACE: Monowi, Nebraska
THE POPULATION: 1
Monowi's sole resident doubles as the town's mayor and librarian.

①

②

THE PLACE:
Gross, Nebraska
THE POPULATION: 2
Once boasting a population of 600, a pair of massive fires in 1909 and 1919 took out many of Gross's businesses and homes, and the town never recovered.

③

THE PLACE:
Buford, Wyoming
THE POPULATION: 1
In 2012, a wealthy businessman bought Buford for $900,000 and renamed it Phin-Deli Town Buford.

④

THE PLACE: Freeport, Kansas
THE POPULATION: 5
Some of the only buildings found in Freeport include a (now-closed) bank built in 1902, a grain elevator, and a church.

The word was out: There was gold—and silver, and other precious minerals—in the hills of the western U.S. and Alaska. Seeking their own stash of that shiny prize, thousands of people descended on the West in the mid- to late 1800s, from California to Colorado, from Wyoming to Alaska.

The Wild West was wild for gold. And, almost overnight, dozens of tiny towns popped out of nowhere. What were once sprawling fields by quiet streams and rushing rivers turned into bustling communities with homes, schools, post offices, shops, churches, and theaters. As more and more miners made their way west, these towns swelled, some seeing populations that soared up to 10,000 people in less than 20 years.

For a while, it seemed that almost anyone with a pick and a pan could strike it rich. In 1852, at the height of the rush, miners collected a jaw-dropping $81 million worth of gold—more than $2 billion in today's dollars. Sam Brannan, a legend of the gold rush, became a millionaire simply selling supplies to miners from his stores throughout California. The West, it seemed, was glittering in gold.

But the gold rush did not last forever. And after so much aggressive mining, a lack of gold and hope of better prospects forced residents to move to other parts of the West, helping to populate cities like San Francisco and Los Angeles. Those who chose to stay where they were struggled to sustain a living in these off-the-beaten-track locations, often set too far away from highways and bigger towns to bring in business.

Over time, some of these mining towns were completely knocked down and developed into suburbs. Others have been turned into tourist attractions, their crumbling buildings and ramshackle homes giving us a glimpse into a life and time so very long ago.

5

THE PLACE:
Weeki Wachee, Florida
THE POPULATION: 12
Weeki Wachee is famous for its live mermaid show, featuring humans dressed as the sea creatures swimming around in a giant tank.

6

THE PLACE:
Tortilla Flat, Arizona
THE POPULATION: 6
You can order a scoop of prickly pear gelato at Tortilla Flat's country store.

7

THE PLACE:
Funkley, Minnesota
THE POPULATION: 5
The mayor of the town passes out "Funkley Bucks" to visitors, which can be used at the restaurant he owns.

8

THE PLACE:
Chicken, Alaska
THE POPULATION: 6 (estimated); varies based on the season. There's no electricity or running water in Chicken.

Bizarre BEACHES

THE WORLD'S COOLEST COASTLINES OFFER SO MUCH MORE THAN JUST SANDY SHORES.

1 HAVING A BALL

WHAT: Bowling Ball Beach

WHERE: Mendocino County, California, U.S.A.

WHY IT'S BIZARRE: Resembling oversize bowling balls, the round stones that line the sand in this state park are also known as **concretions**, or buildups of minerals in the water, eventually exposed by sea erosion.

THERE'S A SIMILAR BOULDER BEACH ON THE COAST OF NEW ZEALAND—THE STONES THERE ARE THOUGHT TO BE 56 MILLION YEARS OLD!

2 HIDE AND BEACH

WHAT: Hidden Beach

WHERE: Marieta Islands, Mexico

WHY IT'S BIZARRE: It's believed that this under-the-radar beach—tucked **inside a crater**—was formed after the roof collapsed on a military site from the early 1900s. It's so secluded you can only reach it by first swimming through a 40-foot (12-m)-long rock tunnel.

5 FOR THE BIRDS
WHAT: Boulders Beach
WHERE: Simon's Town, South Africa
WHY IT'S BIZARRE: Penguins ... at the beach? Flocks of the endangered African penguins splash on the shores and bounce about this national park's famed **540-million-year-old granite boulders.**

8 GLASS FROM THE PAST
WHAT: Glass Beach
WHERE: Fort Bragg, California, U.S.A.
WHY IT'S BIZARRE: Decades ago, the water along this beach was a dumping ground for glass bottles and other debris. What was tossed in the ocean has now washed up as a rainbow of **shimmering sea glass** covering the coves.

THE SEA GLASS AT GLASS BEACH IS SOMETIMES REFERRED TO AS "MERMAID TEARS."

4 BLACK OUT
WHAT: Punalu'u Black Sand Beach
WHERE: Big Island, Hawaii, U.S.A.
WHY IT'S BIZARRE: The jet-black sand on this skinny stretch of beach isn't actually sand: It's tiny bits of **hardened lava,** produced over centuries by the nearby (and still active) Kilauea Crater. This spot is a popular nesting place for hawksbill and green sea turtles.

7 TIP OFF
WHAT: Zlatni Rat
WHERE: Bol, Croatia
WHY IT'S BIZARRE: This **idyllic, narrow beach** on the Croatian coast is a real shape-shifter. Its tip—which sticks out as much as 1,640 feet (500 m) into the ocean—shifts in different directions as a result of wind, waves, and currents.

3 TICKLED PINK
WHAT: Pink Sand Beach
WHERE: Harbour Island, The Bahamas
WHY IT'S BIZARRE: Crushed-up coral, clams, and other small-shelled invertebrates create a **grainy, pale pink sand** that covers stretches of shore on Harbour Island, Bahamas. Pink sand beaches can also be found in Bermuda, Indonesia, Crete, and the Seychelles Islands in the Indian Ocean.

6 BLUE LAGOON
WHAT: Genipabu
WHERE: Natal, Brazil
WHY IT'S BIZARRE: Somewhere between Brazil's tallest sand dunes you'll find these **fresh-water lagoons,** their deep blue water setting a stark contrast against the white peaks. Looking for adventure? Leap from a trapeze on the dunes into the sparkling water below.

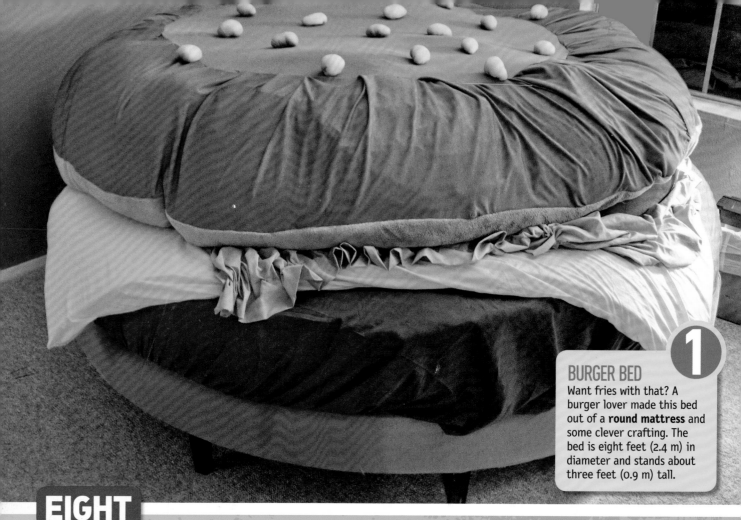

1

BURGER BED
Want fries with that? A burger lover made this bed out of a **round mattress** and some clever crafting. The bed is eight feet (2.4 m) in diameter and stands about three feet (0.9 m) tall.

OUT-OF-THE-BOX BEDS

FROM KOOKY KINGS TO QUIRKY QUEENS, CHECK OUT SOME OF THE WEIRDEST PLACES TO REST YOUR HEAD. SWEET DREAMS!

2

PERFECT POD
Travel may make you weary, but rest assured that you'll be able to fight jet lag with a quick snooze in a **sleep pod.** Popping up at major airports, these capsules can be booked by the hour, allowing you a private—and quiet—spot to squeeze in a catnap.

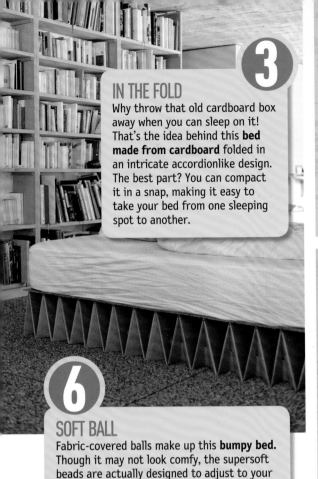

3 IN THE FOLD

Why throw that old cardboard box away when you can sleep on it! That's the idea behind this **bed made from cardboard** folded in an intricate accordionlike design. The best part? You can compact it in a snap, making it easy to take your bed from one sleeping spot to another.

4 DRIVE TIME

Cruise into a good night's sleep in one of the unique automotive-themed rooms at the **V8 Hotel** in Stuttgart, Germany. In this retro bed—a converted Cadillac Coupe de Ville—you can snooze under a starry sky at the drive-in cinema.

5 FEATHER YOUR NEST

Snuggle up in this **circular, nature-inspired** bed and you'll be as cozy as a baby bird. With giant, soft pillows and a wide space for snuggling, this is one nest you might never want to leave.

> COST FOR ONE OF THE WORLD'S MOST EXPENSIVE BEDS? $175,000.

6 SOFT BALL

Fabric-covered balls make up this **bumpy bed.** Though it may not look comfy, the supersoft beads are actually designed to adjust to your body position as you move around, allowing you to sink into a deep and peaceful sleep.

> EACH BED FEATURES 120 BALLS LINKED WITH ELASTIC BANDS, MAKING IT FLEXIBLE ENOUGH TO FOLD INTO ANY POSITION.

7 BRANCHING OUT

You'll really go out on a limb when you sleep on this **four-poster bed.** Handcrafted out of iron, each post resembles a thin tree trunk, their branches meeting in the middle to support a bird's nest. Want one of your own? Better start saving: These tree beds start at $22,500.

8 SO TWISTED

Give your sleepy time a twist by lying down on this **spiral-shaped mattress.** Part of an exhibit by a team of Cuban artists, this bed is said to represent the often twisted and complex connection between sleep and dreams.

EIGHT SUPERSIZE SCULPTURES

THESE JUMBO STATUES ARE TRULY LARGER-THAN-LIFE!

BIG BUDDHAS 2
These colossal statues can be found in Myanmar, a country in Southeast Asia. The standing sculpture stretches 423 feet (129 m) tall, making it one of the **biggest Buddhas** on Earth.

IN THE SWIM 1
A **46-foot (14-m)-long swimmer** strokes along the grassy banks of the Thames River in London, England. The temporary statue—made of Styrofoam hand-painted to resemble real flesh—was set up in the British capital to promote a TV show.

THUMB'S UP 3
The artist who created this **four-story thumb** found in Paris's La Défense district cast it from an impression of his own thumb and fingerprint. Now, where's the rest of his hand?

ROCK STAR **4**

In Romania, the hills have eyes ... and a nose, mouth, and bushy beard. This **gigantic stone sculpture**—carved into a rock wall near the Danube River—represents Decebal, a mighty ruler from ancient times. Some 130 feet (40 m) high, it's the tallest rock sculpture in Europe.

IT TOOK TEN YEARS TO BUILD **DECEBAL.**

HORSING AROUND **5**

A pair of **steel horse heads** greet visitors in Falkirk, Scotland. You can actually enter the sculptures—known as "Kelpies," the name of the working horses that once pulled barges in the area—to admire the artwork from the inside out.

7

REALLY HIGH HEEL

Cinderella would never be able to leave this super-size shoe behind! A Portuguese artist used stainless-steel pots and lids to create a colossal version of the famed **fairy tale slipper.**

TOP BRASS **6**

Perched high on a hill, this 160-foot (49-m)-tall bronze monument of a man, woman, and child overlooks the Atlantic Ocean in Dakar, Senegal. The **tallest statue in Africa,** it marks the country's independence from French rule.

HEAD'S ABOVE THE REST **8**

What a big head you have! This **10-story-tall bust** of communist leader Mao Zedong looms large over the south-central Chinese city of Changsha. More than 8,000 pieces of granite were used to create the mammoth statue.

1

GO FISH
WHAT: Seaglass Carousel
WHERE: New York, New York, U.S.A.
WHY IT'S MAGICAL: The carousel's iridescent, **fiberglass fish figures** are all made to look like sea glass. You can catch a ride on a lionfish, an angelfish, and more, all lit by LEDs creating an underwater effect.

EIGHT
MAGICAL MERRY-GO-ROUNDS
THESE CAROUSELS ARE SOME OF THE NEATEST THINGS GOING AROUND.

2

HIGH RIDE
WHAT: Columbia Carousel
WHERE: Santa Clara, California, U.S.A.
WHY IT'S MAGICAL: This **double-decker ride** stands as tall as a 10-story building—making it one of the world's tallest carousels. Take your pick from leaping horses, or hop on a camel, giraffe, lion, tiger, or any of the other animals that make up this merry-go-round's 100-animal menagerie.

EYE SPY
WHAT: Flying Horses Carousel
WHERE: Oak Bluffs, Massachusetts, U.S.A.
WHY IT'S MAGICAL: One of the oldest operating carousels in the U.S., this ride was built in 1876. Each horse is embellished with **real horsehair tails and manes,** and you can spy tiny animals and other objects etched into their glass eyes.

3

GOLD STANDARD
WHAT: Jane's Carousel
WHERE: Brooklyn, New York, U.S.A.
WHY IT'S MAGICAL: Built in 1922 and later damaged in a fire, this carousel is named for the artist who restored the ride to its original glory. Check out the horses' decorative details painted in pure gold—and the ride's **galloping views** of the Manhattan skyline.

5

SKY HIGH
WHAT: The Star Flyer
WHERE: Copenhagen, Denmark
WHY IT'S MAGICAL: Soar **up to 260 feet (80 m)** in the sky and watch people below mill around like ants as you swing and spin at speeds of more than 40 miles an hour (70 km/h).

6

ANIMAL ACTION
WHAT: Dodo Manège
WHERE: Paris, France
WHY IT'S MAGICAL: On this whimsical ride located in Paris's Jardin des Plantes, you can take a spin on an **extinct animal,** like the prehistoric horned turtle or the dodo bird, or hop on an endangered species, like a panda or gorilla.

7

CALIFORNIA LOVE
WHAT: San Francisco Carousel
WHERE: San Francisco, California, U.S.A.
WHY IT'S MAGICAL: This carousel's come a long way from Italy, where it was originally built. Today the ride is clearly Californian, featuring **hand-painted images** of San Francisco landmarks like the Golden Gate Bridge, Lombard Street, and Chinatown.

8

SOUND THE TRUMPETS!
WHAT: King Julien's Beach Party-Go-Round
WHERE: Sentosa, Singapore
WHY IT'S MAGICAL: They like to move it move it! Part of Universal Studios Singapore, this *Madagascar*-themed merry-go-round features all of the characters from the hit movie spinning around to upbeat dance music.

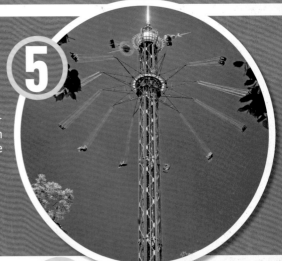

MOST COLORFUL

CORNERS OF THE EARTH

NO FILTER NEEDED! THESE BRIGHT SPOTS AROUND THE WORLD ROCK ALL-NATURAL HUES.

10,000-YEAR-OLD HUMAN REMAINS HAVE BEEN FOUND IN THE HORNOCAL MOUNTAIN RANGE.

RAINBOW ROCKS

2

A rainbow of rock layers glows in fiery shades of orange and red plus purples and pinks. The natural zigzag formations in Argentina's **Hornocal mountain range** appear to change color depending on the shade of the sky.

RAINBOW ROW

1

Tulips grow in neat rows in Holland, where millions of the buds pop up each spring. Originally a wildflower from Asia, tulips were brought to Europe by a botanist in the 17th century. Today, billions of tulips are exported from the Netherlands every year.

MARBLE MARVEL

3

Thanks to centuries of erosion, the underbelly of this towering rock formation found in Chile's **General Carrera Lake** is pure marble. Known as Capillas de Marmol ("Marble Caves"), the caves feature swirling details in the white rock that appear blue as they reflect the glacier-fed lake.

SHADE SHIFTERS

5

You never know what you're going to get when looking at crater lakes in Indonesia's **Kelimutu National Park.** Because of chemical reactions triggered by volcanic activity, the crater lakes are constantly changing color, from navy blue to emerald green to shocking white.

SUPER FLY

4

The gorgeous **Fly Geyser** in Nevada, U.S.A., was the accidental outcome of humans drilling for geothermic energy. But its radiant reddish green glow is all natural—a result of being covered by colorful algae that grow only at extreme temperatures.

CRIMSON TIDE

6

This wetland has visitors *sea*-ing red! China's **Panjin Red Beach** is covered by masses of seepweed, a plant that turns a scarlet shade each autumn. The result? Crimson as far as the eye can see.

BRIGHT BLOOMS

7

Each spring, a carpet of pink wildflowers surrounds the base of Japan's **Mount Fuji.** Tourists flock to the mountain for the annual Festival of Flowers, where they can view the blooms—also known as moss phlox—growing in stunning shades of magenta and blush.

PANJIN RED BEACH IS THE WORLD'S LARGEST WETLAND.

COOL CORAL

8

Dive into Australia's **Great Barrier Reef** and you'll be welcomed into the world's most amazing aquarium: Thousands of coral and tropical fish in an array of bold colors stretch for more than 1,400 miles (2,253 km), creating the world's largest living ecosystem.

Adorably UGLY ANIMALS

WHEN IT COMES TO THESE PECULIAR-LOOKING CREATURES, THERE'S MORE THAN MEETS THE EYE.

BY A NOSE

What a big nose you have! The **proboscis monkey's** huge schnoz—the largest of any primate—can grow to be up to a quarter of the animal's body length. But that peculiar protrusion doesn't stop these creatures from being some of the quickest swimmers in the jungles of Borneo: Webbed feet and hands help them out-paddle predators like crocodiles.

①

44

GENTLE GIANT

With a manatee's body and a whale's tail, a **dugong** looks like a peculiar mash-up of mammals. These slow-moving sea-dwellers—typically found in warm waters from Africa to Australia—are harmless, preferring a diet of sea grass.

OUT OF THE SHELL

What's the matter with the **mata-mata turtle?** Nothing, really—unless you count its bizarre needle nose, bumpy body, and long, flat head. Commonly found in the Amazon River, these turtles have killer camo and are often mistaken for a pile of leaves and mud.

SCIENTISTS ARE WORKING TO SAVE THE KAKAPO FROM EXTINCTION BY SEQUENCING THIS BIRD'S GENETIC CODE.

DEEP FREEZE

With its permanent frowny face and lumpy body, the endangered **blobfish** is one of the weirdest-looking animals out there. Mostly found off the coast of Australia and Tasmania, the fish has been voted the official mascot of the Ugly Animal Preservation Society.

BIRD UP

There are just about 125 **kakapos** left in New Zealand—the only place on the planet where you can find these flightless birds. With their mossy green feathers and plump bodies, kakapos look more like owls than parrots. Another rare feature? They smell like honey. Sweet!

SKIN AND BONES

Whether it's their hairless, pinkish skin, their protruding front teeth, or the fact that they eat each other's poop, **naked mole rats** certainly aren't going to win any beauty competitions. But the wrinkly rodents are valued in the medical world: Highly resilient to cancer, they're helping scientists research a cure for the disease.

MUGLY RECENTLY TOOK THE TITLE AT A WORLD'S UGLIEST DOG CONTEST.

ODD DUCK

Muscovy ducks are recognizable by the wartlike red growths that cover most of their face. But it's only the male Muscovy—which grows to be twice as big as the female—that sports this distinguishing mask. Females get off wart free.

DOGGONE UGLY

With patchy bald skin, stringy white whiskers, and beady eyes, **Mugly, a Chinese crested,** is world-famous for his less-than-perfect appearance. The pup, who lives in Peterborough, England, was even picked to turn on the Christmas lights at Parliament.

TURN THE PAGE FOR MORE INCREDIBLE INFO ABOUT UGLY ANIMALS!

UGLY, EXPLAINED

EIGHT MORE AWESOMELY UGLY ANIMALS

1 AYE-AYE

2 CELESTIAL-EYE GOLDFISH

3 BAIRD TAPIR

4 BLACK SEADEVIL ANGLERFISH

They may not be pretty, but some animals' funky features give them an edge in the wild. Here's how a few of the oddest-looking animals' attributes increase their odds of survival.

THE NOSE KNOWS

A male proboscis monkey's mega-nose isn't just for show. Scientists think these oversize organs create an echo chamber that increases the loudness of the monkey's call, helping it impress females and threaten rival males.

DIG IT

The naked mole rat's giant chompers double as tools to help it dig the deep underground tunnels this animal calls home. And as for that smooth, hairless skin? It's better for quickly wriggling through those passages, keeping it safe from predators like eagles and larger mammals.

LONG STRETCH

The matamata turtle's extra-long neck lets the bottom-dweller come up for air while it stays put on the bottom of the stream. And when a tasty fish swims by? The turtle simply sticks out its neck to nab the fish before swallowing it whole.

SNOUT AND ABOUT

Seeking most of its meals in underwater grasses, a dugong uses its bristled, fleshy snout to root around while its rough lips help it chomp the occasional crab. And as for that whale-like tail? A dugong—which can stay underwater for six minutes—will "stand" on it to raise its head above the surface.

5

GIANT ANTEATER

6

SPHYNX CAT

MARABOU STORK

7

8

STAR-NOSED MOLE

Wildest **EIGHT** RACES

GET READY FOR SOME OF THE MOST EXTREME HEAD-TO-HEAD COMPETITIONS OUT THERE. ON YOUR MARK, GET SET, GO!

THE ANTARCTIC ICE MARATHON IS THE SOUTHERN-MOST MARATHON ON EARTH.

1 WILD MILES
WHAT: The Big Five Marathon
WHERE: Limpopo Province, South Africa
WHY IT'S WILD: Like a **safari on foot**, this race runs through Entabeni Game Reserve in the South African savanna. Take in epic scenery as you stride alongside the "big five" animals—elephants, rhinos, buffaloes, lions, and leopards—plus antelopes, zebras, and more.

2 ICE RUN
WHAT: Antarctic Ice Marathon
WHERE: Union Glacier, Antarctica
WHY IT'S WILD: In the only race held within the Antarctic Circle, runners brave **frosty and fierce conditions** to complete this marathon each November. The average wind chill temp at the start of the race? A frigid minus 4°F (-20°C).

5 GREAT ESCAPE
WHAT: Zombie Run
WHERE: Locations around the world
WHY IT'S WILD: Run for your life! In these eccentric events, **"zombies"** (actually regular people in costume) chase after runners, who must navigate obstacles while they attempt to escape the undead.

8 COSTUME PARTY
WHAT: Mascot Grand National
WHERE: Cambridgeshire, England
WHY IT'S WILD: **Mascots** representing sports teams and businesses went toe-to-toe (or paw-to-paw) in this 200-meter sprint. The reward for finishing first? Bragging rights throughout Great Britain.

IN THE RACE'S NEARLY 40-YEAR HISTORY, ONLY ONE HUMAN HAS BEAT A HORSE.

4 HORSING AROUND
WHAT: Man vs. Horse
WHERE: Llanwrtyd Wells, Wales
WHY IT'S WILD: Think you can **outrun a horse?** You can test your speed at this race, where runners try to outstride horses and their riders over a rolling, 22-mile (35-km) course.

7 ON TRACK
WHAT: Great Sonoma County Handcar Races
WHERE: Santa Rosa, California, U.S.A.
WHY IT'S WILD: Drivers of **human-powered railroad cars**—also known as handcars—show off their stuff (and speed) at this off-the-rails event. From vintage pilots to colorful clowns, entrants dress to match the theme of their creative cars.

3 GOING DOWN
WHAT: Megavalanche
WHERE: Alpe d'Huez, France
WHY IT'S WILD: It's complete chaos as a field of more than **2,000 mountain bikers** careen down the snow-and-ice-covered Pic Blanc, a 10,827-foot (3,300-m) glacier in the French Alps.

6 TAKE A LEAP
WHAT: Skydive Ultra Run
WHERE: Clewiston, Florida, U.S.A.
WHY IT'S WILD: As if running an **extreme 200-mile (322-km) race** in Florida's heat isn't daring enough, competitors in this kooky competition must first leap out of an airplane from 13,500 feet (4,115 m) above the ground.

NO STRINGS ATTACHED

A music-lover *orchestrated* the design for this **violin-shaped pool** in his backyard. At night, 5,600 fiber-optic cables light up like multicolored strings in time to music. A hot tub serves as the violin's chin rest, and the bow is made up of two narrow fish ponds. Bravo!

THIS POOL SHIMMERS WITH MORE THAN 400,000 SHINY GLASS TILES LINING THE BOTTOM AND SIDES.

EIGHT
COOLEST POOLS

SUIT UP AND DIVE IN TO SOME OF THE WORLD'S SPLASHIEST SWIMMING SPOTS.

REPURPOSED RELAXATION

Here's one way to breathe new life into an **old barge:** Turn it into a pool! This popular pool floats on the Spree River in Berlin, Germany, with a wooden footbridge allowing easy access from the riverbank.

④ CROWD CONTROL

On sweltering summer days, swimmers floating in inner tubes pack this saltwater pool in China's Sichuan Province. The **huge indoor water park**—which also features live musical acts and amusement rides—can hold up to 10,000 people at a time. So much for personal space!

③ SKY DIVE

Talk about living in luxury: Some apartments at a condo in Mumbai, India, offer **balcony pools.** Just don't move in if you're afraid of heights: The glass-enclosed pools are a dizzying 37 stories up!

BLOOD (RED) BATH

The water in the **Red Pool** at the Library Hotel in Thailand may look a bit freaky, but fear not: The scarlet hue comes from the deep red, orange, and yellow tiles lining the bottom of the pool.

⑦ OVER THE EDGE

The pool at the Joule Hotel in Dallas, Texas, U.S.A., really leaves it all hanging out there—eight feet (2.4 m) out there, to be exact. One side of the swimming spot juts out from the **edge of the hotel**, offering guests a unique way to check out the city below.

⑥ OFF THE DEEP END

Longer than 20 Olympic-size pools and up to 115 feet (46 m) deep in spots, this **supersize pool** outside of the San Alfonso del Mar resort in Chile holds 66 million gallons (250 million L) of water. It's so big, many visitors opt to make their way from end to end in a sailboat!

⑧ INFINITY AND BEYOND

It may not be the top of the world, but it'll sure feel like it! When you hang out in this **rooftop pool** in Singapore—57 floors up—you're eye-to-eye with some of the city's tallest skyscrapers.

51

EIGHT PIECES OF FAR-OUT FOOTWEAR

TAKE A WALK IN THESE INNOVATIVE AND OUT-THERE SHOES AND ACCESSORIES.

2 LIGHT BRIGHT

Headed out for a run after dark? Strap these **extra-bright accessories** on your sneakers and you'll be good to, uh, glow. Lightweight LED lights attach to the top of each shoe, providing up to 30 feet (9 m) of visibility.

> YADAV HAS ALSO CREATED CUSTOM CARS SHAPED LIKE A TUBE OF LIPSTICK AND A SOCCER BALL.

1 SHOE CAR

Lace up and enjoy the ride in this **custom car!** Indian inventor Sudhakar Yadav cobbled together this vehicle, which features all of the basic functions of a normal car and can reach speeds of up to 28 miles an hour (45 km/h).

3 SO APPEALING

Made from molded leather in a bright yellow hue, this **fruity heel** is the work of designer Kobi Levi, who has also created shoes resembling steaming pots of coffee, swans, and even instruments. Bananas!

SMART SOLES
4

This is one **smart shoe!** Lace up a pair of Greats and the Bluetooth-enabled smart tag in the sole gives you access to an exclusive app on your phone—and allows you to interact with other people wearing the same shoes.

SHOCK VALUE
5

The complex system on the outside of this shoe is meant to **absorb and store the shock** of your body weight with every step you take. This not only makes running easier on your legs and joints, but you also get an added boost with every step.

A SINGLE SHOE TAKES ABOUT SIX HOURS TO PRINT.

IN PRINT
7

You're heading out to a fancy party and don't have any shoes to go with your outfit. Thanks to advancements in **3D printing,** you can have the perfect pair—like these purple wedges—in no time. Customized shoes, in just your size? That's a step in the right direction.

A TRUE VISION
6

This revolutionary shoe just may allow the **visually impaired** to walk without a cane. The still-in-concept design features sensors built into the sole, which vibrates when the wearer approaches objects, including animals and other people.

SPRING FORWARD
8

Foot pain, be gone! Using a system of **rubber balls and springs,** one designer created this helpful heel, which is supposed to make you feel like you're walking on air. That's one way to put a spring in your step!

① FLASH DANCER

One of three colorful new peacock spider species discovered in 2015 in eastern Australia, **Sparklemuffin** *(Maratus jactatus)* makes up for its tiny size (it's smaller than your pinkie fingernail!) with a brightly colored midsection and eye-catching dance that it uses to attract mates.

EIGHT

SENSATIONAL SPIDERS

THESE EIGHT-LEGGED CRAWLERS PROVE SPIDERS CAN BE COOL, CREEPY, OR EVEN … CUTE?

② TWINKLE TOES

Mirror spiders, also known as **sequined spiders** (part of the genus *Thwaitesia*), use special crystals under the skin of their abdomens to reflect light. These adorned arachnids confuse their predators and put on a pretty show for bystanders—fancy!

GREAT BITE
The **Goliath bird-eating tarantula** is one spider you don't want to tangle with! This enormous arachnid inflicts its poisonous bite with one-inch (2.5-cm) fangs and can use projectile body hairs to irritate the eyes, nose, and mouth of any mammal that dares to get too close. And ... did we mention it's big enough to eat a bird?

4

5

SIGNS OF AUTUMN
3

Trick-or-treat! The **pumpkin spider** (*Araneus trifolium*) thrives in places like the United States, England, and Russia. It is typically spotted on a round "orb" garden web in the fall, when its bulbous belly turns from brown or gold to orange.

YOU GONNA EAT THAT?
Burned hamburger patty? Charred marshmallow? Dog poo? Whatever this **bird dung crab spider** reminds you of, it's not likely to be appetizing. But that's just what the spider is counting on as it uses creepy camouflage to evade predators.

7

NO BONES ABOUT IT
Sporting white-on-black stripes, the aptly named **Skeletorus** (*Maratus sceletus*), is another newly discovered peacock spider species found in eastern Australia. This spooky spider doesn't wait on a web for prey; instead, it tackles its meal.

I'M STUMPED
6

The **tree stump orb weaver spider** (*Poltys illepidus*) is active at night, busily tending its orblike web. During the day, though, it remains motionless—disguised as a knobby broken branch with legs tucked tightly against its body.

SEEING SPOTS
A ladybug look-alike, the **ladybird spider** (*Eresus sandaliatus*) lives primarily in England, where its population is protected. In 1993 there were only about 50 spiders left in the U.K., but, because of a captive breeding program, the spiders are making a comeback.

8

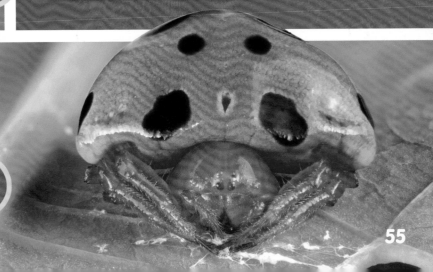

CRAZY-COOL CLOSE-UPS

REAL LIFE LOOKS LIKE SCIENCE FICTION WHEN YOU CATCH A GLIMPSE AT CLOSE RANGE.

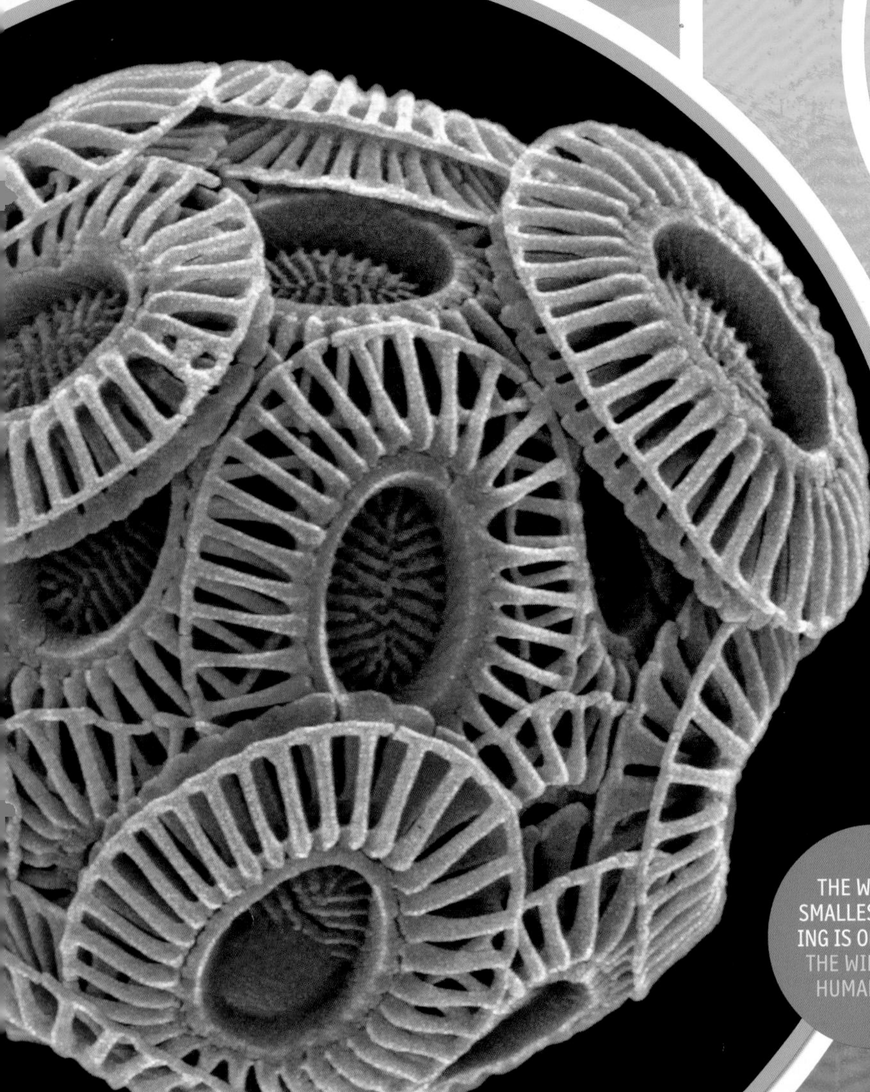

2

FUZZY FIGURES
This isn't dead grass on the front lawn or split ends in need of a trim. It's a close-up view of an **owl feather,** which branches into wavy barbules and happens to be made of keratin, similar to the protein found in human hair.

THE WORLD'S SMALLEST PAINTING IS ONE-THIRD THE WIDTH OF A HUMAN HAIR.

1

THE TINIEST SEASHELLS
They may look like piles of hubcaps at the junkyard, but those discs are actually **coccolithophores,** phytoplankton that hide inside a hard shell only .0001 inch (.003 mm) in diameter and built from the same chemicals that make up limestone.

3

WAR OF THE WORLDS
Part spaceship, part robot invader? This ominous structure isn't a prop from the latest end-of-the-world blockbuster film: It's a **bacteriophage,** a virus that likes to infect bacteria and replicate inside them. The capsule at the top, which holds virus DNA, is less than one-thousandth the width of a human hair.

GIVING THE HAIRY EYEBALL

This image of a **fruit fly eye** taken with a scanning electron microscope shows one feature you'd never see without zooming in so closely: tiny hairs protruding like daggers between the compound lenses.

WATER CYCLE

This is what you'll find in the morning when the temperature drops overnight: **dewdrops.** They transform the world into a sparkly place and draw your eye to wonders you wouldn't notice otherwise, like beaded spiderwebs and leafy hands holding a perfect pearl on the tip of each finger.

NO TWO SNOWFLAKES ARE EXACTLY ALIKE.

CRYSTAL PERFECTION

The intricate details that form in a **snowflake** are all expressed in a surface that's smaller than a coin. These incredible works of art are created through temperature, humidity, and other factors like air pressure that scientists don't quite understand yet.

THAT'S ROUGH

We know sharks have a lot of teeth, but this is ridiculous—these aren't even in its mouth! These barbs, which cover **shark skin,** are each about 150 microns wide. Despite the sandpaper texture, the barbs' true purpose is to decrease turbulence while the shark swims.

COLOR SCALE

Butterfly wings are covered with tiny scales that contain their own pigment, but these scales also contain curious structures called gyroids, which bend light—similar to how a prism works, or oil floating on water—to make the wing look iridescent.

DUCK AND RUN

①

Big-wave surfers developed **underwater rock running** to improve their strength, endurance, and mental control during stress. Now fitness fanatics from other sports are picking it up, too. This exercise is risky, though, so better to leave it to the professionals!

THE FIRST OFFICIAL SURFING CONTEST WAS HELD IN CALIFORNIA, U.S.A., IN 1928.

EIGHT

WACKY WAYS TO **WORK OUT**

SUIT UP AND GET READY TO CHECK OUT THESE ZANY WAYS PEOPLE STAY FIT.

②

FLIPPING OUT

Strength training gets real with **tire flips,** which combine the action of common weight-lifting moves with a tractor tire that can weigh as much as 600 pounds (270 kg). Now that's one heavy haul!

UNDER THE BIG TOP

If you like to clown around, then a **circus arts** class may be just right for you. These classes teach students how to fly on the trapeze, juggle, walk a tightrope, unicycle, spin plates, walk on stilts, and entertain crowds with silly dress-up routines.

4

CATCHY STEPS

3

If someone wants to "catch up" with a **joggler,** should they match the pace of their feet as they jog, the movement of their hands as they juggle, or both? There's so much coordination required for this sport, it boggles (joggles?) the mind!

CAREFUL STEPS

Next time someone calls you a "slacker," take it as a compliment—if you know how to walk a **slackline!** All you need for this balance challenge is the nylon line itself—which can mount low to the ground between trees or poles and is about two inches (5 cm) wide—and a soft place to land.

5

7

OM ON THE WATER

Paddleboard yoga might look like a day at the beach, but this is one wicked watery workout. The tippy platform teaches your body balance and increases core strength, and if you lose focus, you're in for an unexpected swim.

KICK IT OVER THE NET

6

What's more athletic than soccer ... or volleyball ... or karate? How about a wildly popular Asian kickball sport that combines all three in what is called **sepak takraw.** Some kicks involve cartwheels, while others look more like flips.

NINJA STYLE

Parkour practitioners (called traceurs) run up walls, pounce on stair rails, and swing or somersault just about anywhere. The mental and physical challenge is about looking for a fun, fast path through an obstacle course.

8

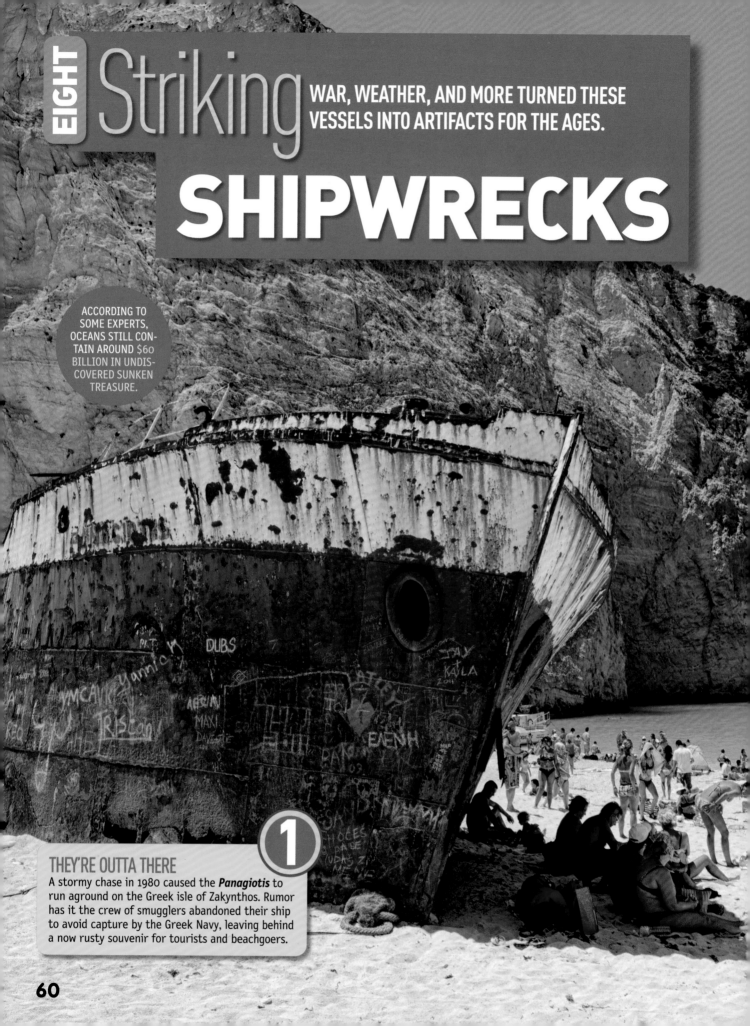

EIGHT Striking

WAR, WEATHER, AND MORE TURNED THESE VESSELS INTO ARTIFACTS FOR THE AGES.

SHIPWRECKS

ACCORDING TO SOME EXPERTS, OCEANS STILL CONTAIN AROUND $60 BILLION IN UNDISCOVERED SUNKEN TREASURE.

① THEY'RE OUTTA THERE

A stormy chase in 1980 caused the *Panagiotis* to run aground on the Greek isle of Zakynthos. Rumor has it the crew of smugglers abandoned their ship to avoid capture by the Greek Navy, leaving behind a now rusty souvenir for tourists and beachgoers.

2

HIGH AND DRY

What happens when you stop a river? These boats, moored in what's known as the **Aral Ship Graveyard,** show one potential pitfall: They're all that's left of a small fishing community in Uzbekistan that was abandoned when the former Soviet Union diverted river water to irrigate crops.

HIDDEN GIANT

Though one of the biggest and most heavily armed vessels of her time, the Japanese battleship *Musashi* caught fire and sank after numerous torpedo and bomb hits from U.S. military forces during World War II. *Musashi* remained hidden in darkness for more than 70 years until researchers spotted her in March 2015 near the Philippines.

4

3

IT TAKES ONLY A FEW WEEKS FOR CORALS, ANEMONES, AND SMALL FISH TO START CONVERTING A SHIPWRECK INTO AN ARTIFICIAL REEF.

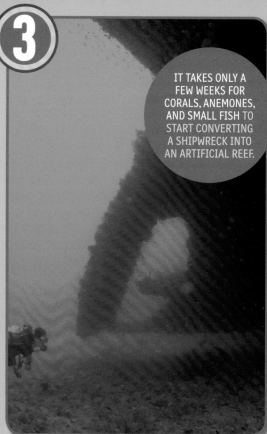

REFUGE IN THE REEF

The steel-built **S.S. *Yongala*,** which sank in the middle of Australia's Great Barrier Reef Marine Park during a 1911 cyclone, is now an underwater refuge for oysters, sea fans, damselfish, and cod. It is also a popular shipwreck for advanced scuba divers to explore.

5

THAR SHE BLOWS!

This former Soviet cargo ship was pulled off course by the 145-mile-an-hour (233-km/h) winds of Hurricane Frances in 2004. Now *La Famille Express* rests as a tourist attraction in shallow water off the coast of Turks and Caicos.

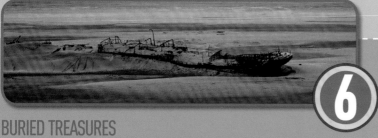

6

BURIED TREASURES

Ships passing Namibia's **Skeleton Coast** have had to withstand thick fog, strong currents, and driving winds that push ships toward shore. Vessels that succumbed to the forces of nature became—and remain—stuck in the sand with their cargo.

8

POINT OF PERIL

Just north of the port of San Francisco, California, U.S.A., **Point Reyes** waits for ships like a treacherous claw, reaching 10 miles (16 km) into the ocean. This rocky coast has witnessed more than 50 shipwrecks and continues to snag small vessels with bad weather, malevolent currents, and jagged shoreline nearly every year.

7

DIGGING FOR HISTORY

Treacherous currents, storms, and sandbars have wrecked an estimated 1,000 ships off of **Hatteras Beach,** in the Outer Banks of North Carolina, U.S.A. Tides and wind pull back the sand for beachgoers and archaeologists who want to explore this "graveyard of the Atlantic."

TURN THE PAGE FOR MORE SHIPWRECKS!

PART OF
THE SHIP
ON DISPLAY

STUCK in TIME

In 2004, a scuba-diving archaeologist swimming in the Rhône River near the city of Arles, in southern France, noticed a strange hunk of wood sticking out of a pile of sunken rubbish. That timber belonged to a 102-foot (31-m) wooden barge that was mostly buried in mud. It also happened to be the most complete Roman shipwreck in history, **preserved for about 2,000 years.**

If the barge had sunk in a warm, salty ocean, the most likely outcome would have been obliteration by wood-eating sea worms. But the Rhône runs with frigid freshwater—not the sort of environment where sea worms hang out. As a result, French archaeologists were able to recover the barge **almost completely intact.** Working in the polluted, murky water, divers hand-sawed the vessel into ten sections that they then carefully lifted to the surface. Scientists soaked the wood in a preservative chemical for several months, freeze-dried and irradiated it to prevent the once waterlogged structure from

collapsing, and then rebuilt the barge plank by plank to its original form.

The complete *Arles-Rhône 3* is now on display in the Musée Départemental de l'Arles Antique, in the town of Arles, along with artifacts discovered nearby in the great Rhône trash heap that hint at what life may have been like in this town two millennia ago: pots that carried olive oil, wine, and fish sauce; women's jewelry and hairpins; a centurion's sword, a bone-handled knife worn on a cord around the neck; and a marble

EIGHT SURPRISING-BUT-TRUE SHIPWRECK FINDS

① A metal alloy thought by some to be evidence of the lost city of Atlantis (circa 2,600 years ago)

② Oregano-infused olive oil (circa 2,400 years ago)

③ An altar (circa 2,200 years ago)

④ Ancient Roman surgical instruments (circa 2,000 years ago)

⑤ A bronze astronomical calculator known as the Antikythera mechanism (circa 2,100 years ago)

⑥ A Viking sunstone, used for navigation (circa 500 years ago)

⑦ 11 million gold coins and jewels (circa 300 years ago)

⑧ Motorcycles, tanks, trucks, and a train engine (from a ship that sank in 1941)

CONSERVING AND RESTORING

RAISING THE WRECK

statue of Julius Caesar, the ruler who conquered this region and turned Arles into an outpost of the Roman Empire.

Most of these artifacts carry no sign of who owned them or why they ended up in the Rhône. But the *Arles-Rhône 3* came to the surface with enough detail to sketch a rough picture of the moments before she went under.

The long narrow boat had once been moored on the bank of Arles, a bustling commercial crossroad town used by the Roman army to transport goods between the northern and southern edges of their empire.

The barge was loaded with 21 tons (19 t) of limestone block that was probably needed at a construction site to the north. But then **a storm rolled in.** The river rose quickly, boiling with strong, muddy currents. The barge wobbled and shivered with the force of it. And then, she sank.

Like a blizzard whirling with snowflakes, the water covered everything beneath its surface with brown silt.

Floating trees barreled down the channel but **the barge stayed safe,** protected by a thickening layer of mud. A thousand years passed, and then another thousand.

Along with the limestone blocks the barge carried, divers found a pot and charcoal the barge crew used to cook meals; a sickle knife they used to chop kindling; and letters burned into her plank—C L POSTU—that could indicate who built the barge, possibly brothers named Caius and Lucius Postumius.

EIGHT
COOL CLOCKS

THESE TERRIFIC TIMEPIECES MERGE ART AND SCIENCE.

TIME MOVES SLOWER IN EARTH'S GRAVITATIONAL FIELD THAN IT DOES IN OUTER SPACE.

TICK, TICK, CHOMP, CHOMP **2**

The **Corpus Clock** in Cambridge, England, combines modern tech and sculpture with classic mechanics. Pacing the perimeter of a rippled gold disc is a chronophage that resembles a grasshopper opening its jaws to gobble each second. The word "chrono-phage" is a combination of the Greek words chronos and phage, meaning "time eater."

BIG TIME **1**

The **Makkah clock tower** in Saudi Arabia is the tallest clock tower in the world. It also holds records for biggest clock face (about 140 feet [40 m] across) with a minute hand that's as long as a tennis court.

GOLDEN GEARS **3**

A Danish locksmith named Jens Olsen designed the **World Clock** in Copenhagen; it has 15,488 parts, many of which are plated in gold. Besides keeping the time in various cities, this cool clock also tracks the moment of sunrise and sunset, future lunar and solar eclipses, and the positions of the planets. Outta this world!

4 PATTERN PLAY

The **Osaka City Station water clock** in Japan uses a computer-controlled curtain of falling water drops to display the time. It also sprays flowers, trees, and musical note patterns for those who can find the time. (Get it?)

5 TIME FLOW

Though it's still a prototype, the **Rhei clock** isn't just a timepiece, it's a work of art. A magnetic liquid flows across the clock face to display digital time in fluid number shapes. Just like your life, every minute is unique!

6 WATER CYCLE

The Children's Museum of Indianapolis in Indiana, U.S.A., hosts this **giant water clock,** which uses a pendulum, a pump, 40 glass pieces, and 70 gallons (265 L) of water mixed with methyl alcohol to give you the time of day.

7 SMELLS LIKE THE RIGHT TIME

Loud buzzers and yappy radio hosts sound like an awful way to start the day. But what about waking up to the aroma of freshly baked croissants, or chocolate, or peppermint? Odor-releasing **Sensorwake** is an "olfactory alarm clock" that releases these and other super smells to rouse you from your slumber.

8 ROLL WITH IT

It's hard to lose track of time while visiting Yokohama Cosmoworld, an amusement park in Japan. Thanks to **Cosmo Clock 21,** a digital timepiece in the center of the park's enormous Ferris wheel, you'll always know whether you have time for one more ride.

THE HUMAN BRAIN HAS A BUILT-IN CLOCK THAT CONTROLS WHEN WE FEEL SLEEPY AND WHEN WE FEEL AWAKE.

EIGHT

Freaky FROGS

HOP TO IT! THESE AMPHIBIANS ARE AMONG
THE MOST UNUSUAL ANIMALS ON EARTH.

A GROUP OF FROGS IS CALLED AN ARMY.

FROGS SHED THEIR SKIN— AND SOMETIMES EAT IT—ABOUT ONCE A WEEK.

② RAD REPUTATION

The **sanguine poison frog** (*Allobates zaparo*) lives in Ecuador and parts of Peru, where it avoids predators by mimicking the red-spotted pattern of other highly toxic frogs. That's pretty smart, because the sanguine frog isn't actually poisonous at all!

① STUCK IN HIS THROAT

Darwin's frog (*Rhinoderma darwinii*) tadpoles are off the menu for insects and fish. Fathers of the species swallow their wriggling babies into their vocal sack, where the kids sprout legs and lose their tail—emerging when they've grown about half an inch (1 cm) in size. Talk about a doting dad!

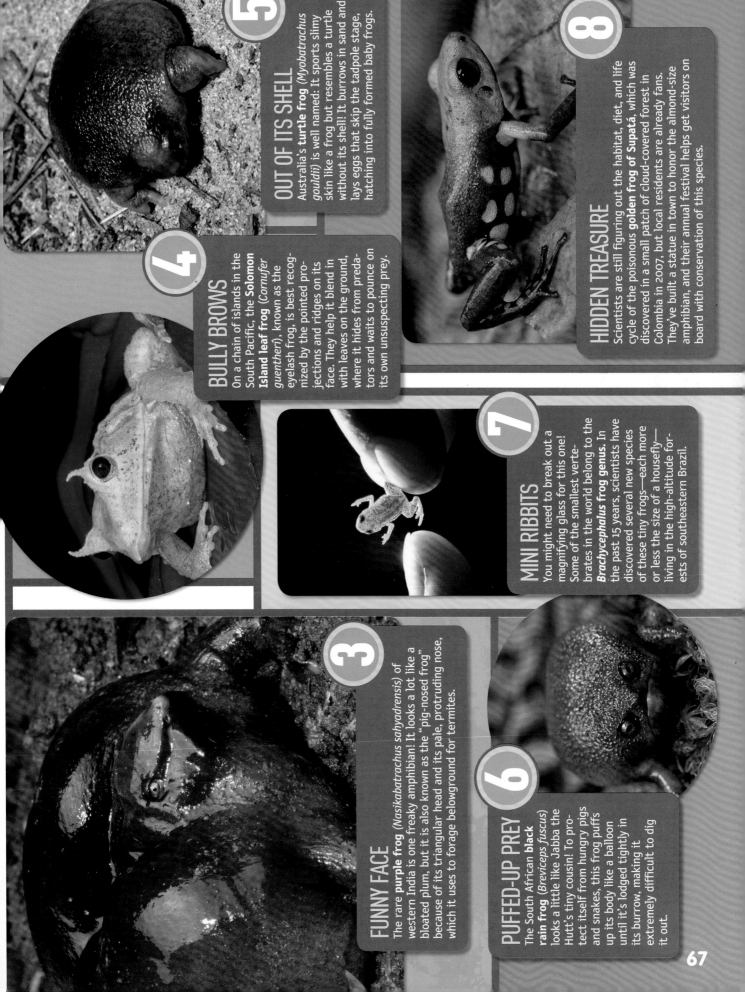

5 OUT OF ITS SHELL

Australia's **turtle frog** (*Myobatrachus gouldii*) is well named: It sports slimy skin like a frog but resembles a turtle without its shell! It burrows in sand and lays eggs that skip the tadpole stage, hatching into fully formed baby frogs.

4 BULLY BROWS

On a chain of islands in the South Pacific, the **Solomon Island leaf frog** (*Cornufer guentheri*), known as the eyelash frog, is best recognized by the pointed projections and ridges on its face. They help it blend in with leaves on the ground, where it hides from predators and waits to pounce on its own unsuspecting prey.

8 HIDDEN TREASURE

Scientists are still figuring out the habitat, diet, and life cycle of the poisonous **golden frog of Supatá**, which was discovered in a small patch of cloud-covered forest in Colombia in 2007, but local residents are already fans. They've built a statue in town to honor the almond-size amphibian, and their annual festival helps get visitors on board with conservation of this species.

7 MINI RIBBITS

You might need to break out a magnifying glass for this one! Some of the smallest vertebrates in the world belong to the **Brachycephalus frog genus.** In the past 15 years, scientists have discovered several new species of these tiny frogs—each more or less the size of a housefly—living in the high-altitude forests of southeastern Brazil.

3 FUNNY FACE

The rare **purple frog** (*Nasikabatrachus sahyadrensis*) of western India is one freaky amphibian! It looks a lot like a bloated plum, but it is also known as the "pig-nosed frog" because of its triangular head and its pale, protruding nose, which it uses to forage belowground for termites.

6 PUFFED-UP PREY

The South African **black rain frog** (*Breviceps fuscus*) looks a little like Jabba the Hutt's tiny cousin! To protect itself from hungry pigs and snakes, this frog puffs up its body like a balloon until it's lodged tightly in its burrow, making it extremely difficult to dig it out.

1
JUMBO SIZE

Swiss origami artist Sipho Mabona folded this **life-size elephant** using a single sheet of 50-foot (15-m)-square paper. Reaching a height of 10 feet (3 m) and weighing in at a whopping 550 pounds (250 kg), the sculpture took four weeks and a team of people to fold.

ORIGAMI CAN BE USED TO SOLVE EQUATIONS IN ALGEBRA.

EIGHT
PIECES OF INCREDIBLE ORIGAMI

IMAGINATION, PATIENCE, AND COUNTLESS CREASES CAN FOLD MAGIC INTO ORDINARY PAPER.

KING OF THE MOUNTAIN

These **gorillas** are the work of Akira Yoshizawa, an origami master whose artistic career spanned more than 50 years. Yoshizawa developed hundreds of new origami patterns and pioneered the wet-folding technique that makes the origami look more like real animals and people.

2

FANTASTIC FIGURES

Your eyes aren't playing tricks on you—that's made of paper! French origami artist Eric Joisel used a wet-folding technique and special paper to create sculptures like this one—called **Three Kings.** With such tiny, detailed, life-like qualities, that truly is outrageous origami!

4

3

WORTH THE WAIT

Advanced origami involves hundreds of steps and intense concentration. But the work doesn't have to be done all at once; you can just set it aside (in a safe, dry place) and try again later. That's what origami expert Robert J. Lang did with **Cactus, Opus 680,** which he finished seven years after having begun!

RULE-BREAKERS

Contrary to the exact, careful folds of traditional origami, members of the zany origami club known as Le Crimp seem to just wing it. They fold and then crumple paper until it magically evolves into amazing sculptures like this one by Eric Vigier, called **Flap of a Butterfly.**

5

7

PUZZLING PATTERNS

Origami like this piece, folded by Eric Gjerde, simply repeats geometric shapes to form what mathematicians call a **tessellation.** The textures that result mimic stars in the sky or scales on a snake (yikes!), flexing, squishing, rolling ... and making it hard to resist the urge to touch!

6

MYTHICAL BEAST

Like something out of a dream, this **unicorn head** sculpture, designed and folded by Vietnamese origami artist Hoang Tien Quyet, uses handmade paper and the technique known as wet folding, in which the paper is moistened to create a curved or wavy effect.

CALCULATED FOLDING

The scaled, slippery-looking **Koi, Opus 425** was designed and folded by Robert J. Lang, who also made a supercool computer program that calculates "crease maps"—or how-to-fold diagrams—for any creature on land, in the air, or under the sea.

8

EIGHT WINNING WAYS TO WORK TOGETHER

IT TAKES TEAMWORK IN THE EXTREME TO PULL OFF THESE PICTURE-PERFECT SHOTS!

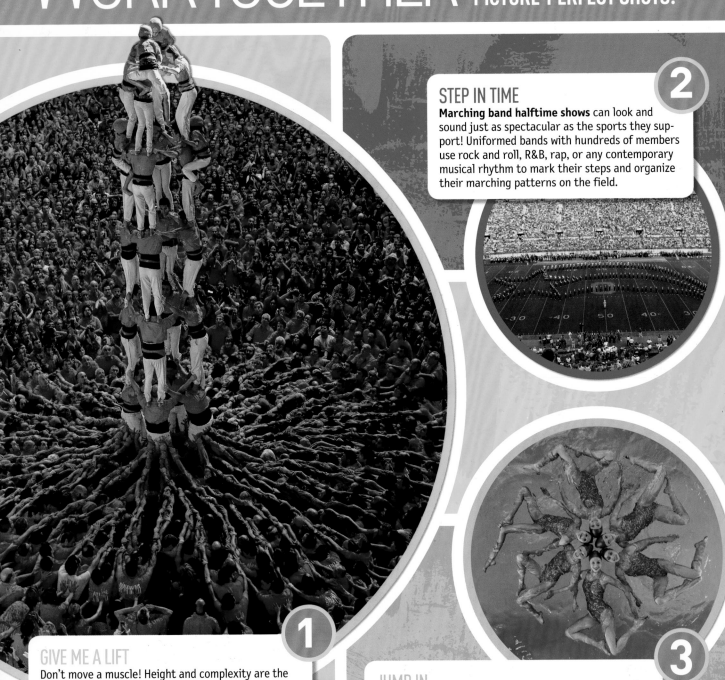

STEP IN TIME
2

Marching band halftime shows can look and sound just as spectacular as the sports they support! Uniformed bands with hundreds of members use rock and roll, R&B, rap, or any contemporary musical rhythm to mark their steps and organize their marching patterns on the field.

GIVE ME A LIFT
1

Don't move a muscle! Height and complexity are the criteria that judges use to determine who wins the **Castell competitions** in Catalonia, Spain, where teams of up to 600 people form a human tower, intertwining their limbs and bodies for strength and balance.

JUMP IN
3

It may look like a sea of arms and legs, but **synchronized swimming** requires serious cool in the pool: These superstrong swimmers have to be able to hold their breath underwater for a minute or more, all while performing a combination of ballet and gymnastics in sync with their teammates—and making sure to smile for the judges.

FLIP OVER THIS

4

In 2011, children in the stands at a stadium in Pyongyang, North Korea, held placards in sync to compose a huge, **people-powered mosaic.**

LET'S BOOGIE

5

If you suddenly hear loud music and see a bunch of strangers take over a public space with choreographed dancing, you're about to be caught up in a **flash mob!** Better step to the side and let the dancers do their thing—these routines may seem spontaneous but are organized (and rehearsed) in advance.

GO TEAM!

6

European football fans (soccer fans in the U.S.) really get into the game with **tifo,** the coordinated display of colored clothes, cards, and large banners that give a boost to their favorite team by sporting a cheer, logo, or larger-than-life mascot.

ON MAY 25, 1986, NEARLY SIX MILLION PEOPLE IN THE UNITED STATES HELD HANDS TO RAISE MONEY FOR CHARITY.

7

FLOWER POWER

To honor soldiers who died during World War I, more than 1,300 students from Bohunt School in England gathered on their campus in 2014 to form the **aerial image** of a poppy flower, a symbol of remembrance for veterans. The students held red papers in the air while a news camera raised on a pole snapped this photo.

8

FREE FALL

Since the parachute was invented in the early 1900s, the sport of **skydiving** has become more intense—and crowded!—every year. Today, large formations of dozens of people holding hands plummet to Earth at speeds approaching 120 miles an hour (200 km/h)!

1

SNUG AS A BUG

Earth shelters channel our early ancestors to make an eco-friendly crash pad: Dig into a hillside and use the surrounding dirt as insulation to cut down on the energy needed for heating and cooling. These shelters work best with sandy soil or gravel, and a domed roof with plenty of windows can make residents as cozy as bunnies in a den.

EIGHT
SWELL DWELLINGS
THESE ENVIRONMENTALLY FRIENDLY STRUCTURES RAISE THE BAR FOR GREEN LIVING.

2

HOMEGROWN

It may look like a straw house, but the Big Bad Wolf would have to huff and puff a long time before he could blow down this super-shelter! Bamboo is among the strongest building materials on the planet, making **bamboo structures** like this school in Bali, Indonesia, a sturdy alternative for people (and little pigs).

THE FIRST PEOPLE TO BUILD PERMANENT HOMES WERE THE NATUFIANS, WHO LIVED IN VILLAGES ON THE EASTERN EDGE OF THE MEDITERRANEAN SEA AROUND 12,000 YEARS AGO.

OFF THE GRID

You choose the location, and **Ecocapsule** has everything else that you need: a wind turbine and rooftop solar panels to store energy for your electronics; a rainwater catchment system to supply the kitchen sink, shower, and toilet; and a fold-up double bed with space-saving closets that maximize 68 square feet (6.3 sq m) of usable living space.

3

HOLE IN THE WALL

4

"Hole in the wall" could mean a small, dingy space ... but it could also be a way to refer to some of the coolest, oldest houses imaginable—**cave homes!** Both naturally formed and man-made, these shelters, still used around the world, are strong, energy-efficient, and easy to maintain.

DIRT DOMES

Build a fireproof, flood-proof, wind-proof home using **Superadobe** technology! The system involves filling long sandbags with dirt, coiling the filled bags, and attaching the layers to one another with barbed wire. A nine-room, double eco-dome design takes about 10 weeks of construction to complete.

5

BUILT BY HAND

Thousands of years ago, Italian peasants made **trullo homes** using limestone boulders stacked without mortar (the stuff that cements bricks in place) so they could be dismantled in a hurry whenever the tax collector rolled into town. Today the trullos are popular tourist attractions, offering vacationers a comfortable and eco-friendly place to stay.

7

NICE THATCH!

6

Popular throughout Europe as well as in East Asian and tropical countries, **thatched houses** are made from the fibrous stalks or leaves of grasses and other plants that grow nearby. When properly installed, thatching offers excellent heat and sound insulation and can last around 50 years before it needs to be replaced.

GET CLOSE TO NATURE

8

In a concrete jungle of sidewalks and skyscrapers, **green walls** like this one can support a climbing ecosystem of sun- and shade-loving plants that will keep the inside of the building cool while exchanging oxygen for carbon dioxide on the outside.

CROWNING GLORY

1

This tiara is literally fit for a princess. The timeless topper, worn by the **Duchess of Cambridge** on her wedding day, features more than 800 diamonds. It was originally made for the Queen of England in 1936.

FEAST YOUR EYES ON SOME OF THE PLANET'S PRICIEST—AND PRETTIEST!— GEMS AND JEWELS.

EIGHT
PIECES THAT
BRING THE BLING

BRACE YOURSELF

This **diamond-encrusted bracelet** is the cat's meow! The panther—dazzling with hundreds of diamonds and an emerald eye—is a signature piece from famed jeweler Cartier. You can get your paws on a similar piece for a cool $46,500.

TRUE BLUE

A Hong Kong billionaire bought this stunner—known as the **Blue Moon diamond**—for his seven-year-old daughter. The price? $48.4 million, making it one of the priciest gemstones ever sold at auction.

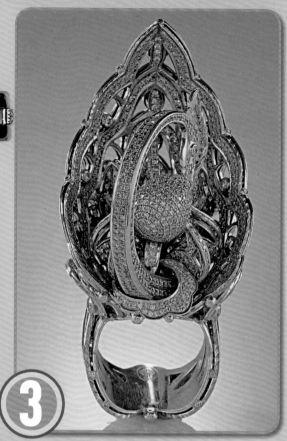

DIAMONDS FOR DAYS

As if one diamond weren't enough, how about 2,525? That's just how many stones make up the **"Tsarevna Swan,"** making it a world record–setting ring. It took jewelers more than 3,600 hours—that's 150 days!—to create this blinged-out bauble.

SEEING RED

This sparkly 26-carat stone—set next to two shield-shaped diamonds—racked up $30 million at an auction. The **extremely rare ruby** is believed to have been found in Mogok, a mining town in Southeast Asia.

THIS STONE IS ALSO KNOWN AS THE SUNRISE RUBY FOR ITS RICH RED HUE.

GOLDEN EGG

Featuring an egg-size yellow diamond hanging from a string of 90 more diamonds on a rose gold chain, this necklace is known as the **"Golden Giant."** Worth $55 million, it's considered the most valuable necklace in the world.

ROCK STAR

This **blue star sapphire**—named after the distinctive star-shaped mark found at its center—is believed to be the world's largest. Discovered in a Sri Lankan mine, the blue bauble is said to be worth a whopping $300 million.

IN THE PINK

The color of bubble gum, this rare rock—nicknamed **"Sweet Josephine"**—recently fetched $28.5 million at auction. At 16 carats, the sparkler is one of the largest pink rocks on the planet.

TURN THE PAGE FOR MORE BLING!

BUSTED! THE TRUE STORY OF A HOLLYWOOD-STYLE JEWEL HEIST

It reads like a page ripped from the script of an upcoming blockbuster movie: A team of longtime bandits plot what would be one of the biggest jewel heists in history. Their plan? To sneak into a safe deposit facility disguised as workmen, disarm the security system, and then drill through a thick cement wall to access the vault—and at least $20 million worth of cash, diamonds, and gems.

The story may sound far-fetched, but that's just what happened in London's Hatton Garden depository in April 2015.

Even more surprising? The gang was made up of members in their 50s, 60s, and 70s! These gray-haired lawbreakers may not be what you picture as bank robbers, but they did get the job done: After spending two days in the vault over a long holiday weekend, the crew managed to casually roll trash cans full of priceless possessions right out and into a getaway car. The crime shocked the city and set Scotland Yard—the United Kingdom's version of the F.B.I.— on high alert.

The thieves' tale, however, did not have a Hollywood ending. Police soon identified the suspects, and, after bugging their car, overheard them bragging about the brazen act. Upon arresting the aged offenders, police discovered some of the stolen goods, including bags of gems that had been stashed in a cemetery.

Today, the Hatton Garden thieves are serving jail sentences—and will be forever remembered as the robbers who almost got away.

EIGHT OF THE PRICIEST JEWELRY HEISTS OF ALL TIME

SMASHED SAFE DEPOSIT BOXES IN THE UNDERGROUND VAULT OF HATTON GARDEN

1 WHERE: Intercontinental Carlton Cannes Hotel, in Cannes, France
WHEN: 2013
ESTIMATED HAUL: $136 million

2 WHERE: Harry Winston Jewelers, in Paris, France
WHEN: 2008
ESTIMATED HAUL: $118 million

3 WHERE: The tarmac of Schiphol Airport, in Amsterdam, The Netherlands
WHEN: 2005
ESTIMATED HAUL: $118 million (from armored trucks)

4 WHERE: Antwerp Diamond Center, in Belgium
WHEN: 2003
ESTIMATED HAUL: $100+ million

5 WHERE: Graff Diamonds, in London, England
WHEN: 2009
ESTIMATED HAUL: $65 million

6 WHERE: ABN Amro Bank, in Antwerp, Belgium
WHEN: 2007
ESTIMATED HAUL: $28 million

7 WHERE: Damiani Showroom, in Milan, Italy
WHEN: 2008
ESTIMATED HAUL: $20 million

8 WHERE: The Museon, in The Hague, The Netherlands
WHEN: 2002
ESTIMATED HAUL: $12 million

RADICAL ROBOTS

YOU'LL BE AMAZED BY WHAT THESE MARVELOUS MACHINES CAN DO!

ONE CUTE COMPUTER

Paro robots, modeled after Canadian harp seals, comfort sick people who feel sad or stressed. The seals blink and make sounds like real animals, and they respond to light, touch, body position, and certain words, including their name.

FUNBOT

ASIMO robot is about the size of a fourth grader, and it definitely captures the spirit of one: It can run, jump, and kick a soccer ball! It can also serve tea, give an office tour, and even make its own decisions, such as whether to make room for someone passing in the hall or whether to re-juice at the battery powering station.

GET A GRIP

If the job is small and the procedure needs to be delicate, these **microrobotic tentacles** are up for the task. Only as long as a grain of rice, and less than a hundredth of an inch (.03 cm) wide, the tiny tentacles spiral around objects to get a grip without squeezing too hard.

HALT! WHO GOES THERE?

This bot means business! **GuardBot**—which can roll across water or up and down hills on land or snow—uses two cameras and can be outfitted with other sensors to watch for trespassers or investigate potentially dangerous situations before humans get too close.

READY RESPONDER

4

Researchers at the NASA Jet Propulsion Lab designed **RoboSimian** as a disaster-response machine. This robot can lift objects, drive a car, open doors, turn off valves, drill through walls, and walk across areas strewn with debris.

SCIENTISTS HAVE INVENTED WARM, ARTIFICIAL SKIN FOR ROBOTS, AND HUMAN TESTERS CAN'T TELL THE DIFFERENCE.

COOL COPILOT

6

After launching the first Kirobo into space as an astronaut travel companion, Toyota designed the tiny **Kirobo Mini** to communicate with drivers and help them stay calm, alert, and safe in their cars. The four-inch (10-cm)-tall robot can read human facial expressions, tone of voice, and body language.

CREEPY CRAWLY

7

Arachnophiles will be delighted by the lifelike appearance and movements of **Robugtix T8,** a tarantula-inspired robot that uses 26 specialized motors to coordinate its head, abdomen, and eight limbs. The T8 can walk, crouch, swivel, and raise itself up as if ready to attack. Just don't confuse it for the real thing!

STUNT DOUBLE

8

The **Yamaha Motobot** has one goal: to ride a motorcycle really, really fast. Its specific challenge is to beat the lap record of Italian moto-racing legend Valentino Rossi— reaching a speed of 124 miles an hour (200 km/h) or more—by the year 2017.

MORE THAN TWO-THIRDS OF OUR PLANET'S FRESHWATER IS STORED IN ICE.

FANTASTIC FROZEN FEATURES

IT'S ALL ABOUT ICE! CHECK OUT THESE COOLER THAN COOL FORMATIONS.

1 COOL CASTLE

The Russian empress Anna Ivanovna is said to have built the first ice palace in 1740 as a cruel joke on one of her relatives, who was supposed to meet her end inside it. Yikes! Today's ice palaces—like this one, **Bonhomme's Ice Palace,** which is built for the Quebec Winter Carnival each year—are more fanciful and meant for shorter-term visits.

2 COLORFUL CAVES

What do you get when geothermal hot springs carve a long channel beneath heavy snow compressed as ice? **Ice caves!** Differences in ice thickness refract light to reveal a full spectrum of colors, with thicker ice appearing blue or green. But don't linger too long— ice caves can collapse at any moment.

SLOW RELEASE

3

Methane gas released from decaying plants or animals gets trapped as **ice bubbles** in freezing surface water. As the temperature drops, the bubbles freeze deeper, creating beautiful columns of gas just waiting to be released in spring. Passersby are sure in for a stinky surprise!

4

THE GREAT SKATE

Each winter a canal in Ottawa, Canada, turns into the world's largest ice rink. When completely frozen, the **Rideau Canal Skateway** has 4.8 miles (7.8 km) of continuous skating surface. It's open to the public, and it's free!

5

ICE AND COZY

In Norway, vacationers at the Kakslauttanen Arctic Resort can stay in snowy **igloos** or in these incredible imitations, which are built from glass and offer a spectacular nighttime view of the aurora borealis from August until April.

FORCE-FUL FREEZEWORK

6

At **ice sculpture** exhibits like this one, held in Belgium in 2015 to celebrate the release of the movie *Star Wars: The Force Awakens,* artists push the limits of what they can achieve with frozen water, adding or removing tiny air bubbles during cool down to control the cloudiness of the ice and using dyes to lend color. With proper care, the finished pieces can last for months.

FREEZE FRAME

Like waterfalls put on pause, **huge icicles** show what happens to lots of dripping water when the air temperature falls faster than the water temperature. If you dare to look up close (careful—icicles can be sharp!), you'll discover they have hollow tips and evenly spaced ripples.

7

FLOWER POWER

8

Delicate ice crystals known as **frost flowers** form on thin sea ice when the atmosphere is colder than the ice underneath. Unlike actual flowers, though, these eye-catching clusters don't thrive in the sunlight!

EIGHT
LIBRARIES YOU'LL LOVE

FROM BEAUTIFUL BUILDINGS TO DARING DESIGNS, HERE ARE SOME UNIQUE PLACES TO CURL UP WITH A GOOD BOOK.

THE U.S. LIBRARY OF CONGRESS **HAS** 838 MILES (1,349 KM) OF SHELVING.

DARING DESIGN

Like an abstract toy block tower, or something designed by Picasso, the steel-and-glass exterior of the **Seattle Central Library** in Washington State, U.S.A., dazzles the eyes with parallel lines, intersections, angles, vertices, and cantilevers.

CHECK IT OUT

Even the outside of the **Kansas City Public Library,** in Missouri, U.S.A., offers visitors reading-list suggestions! Known as the Community Bookshelf, the library's parking garage was decorated in 2004 with two-story-tall book spines showcasing 22 titles nominated by local readers.

GIFT OF READING

The dawn of the age of iron-framed architecture made it possible to construct towering skyscrapers, as well as massive, airy interiors like that of the **George Peabody Library** in Baltimore, Maryland, U.S.A. Built in 1878, the library has a "Stack Room" with five levels of cast-iron balconies that wrap around and are capped by a skylight more than 60 feet (18.3 m) up.

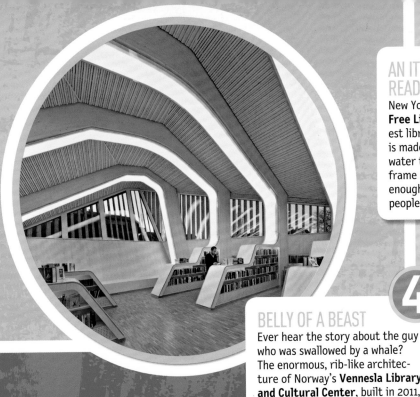

AN ITTY-BITTY READING ROOM

New York City's **Little Free Library,** the smallest library in the world, is made from a recycled water tank and a wooden frame and is large enough for one or two people to fit "inside."

4

BELLY OF A BEAST

Ever hear the story about the guy who was swallowed by a whale? The enormous, rib-like architecture of Norway's **Vennesla Library and Cultural Center,** built in 2011, might make you feel a little like Pinocchio's father Geppetto—or at least inspire you to look for a similar tale on its shelves.

6

RULE BREAKER

This isn't your cookie-cutter reading room. Instead, architects designed **Cottbus Library** in Germany to go against convention, with a cloverleaf exterior shape, a six-story spiral staircase, superbold colors on floors and walls, and an exterior façade decorated with alphabetic symbols from various languages.

7

EXTREME READING

Visitors to this "megalibrary" can wander through its networks of balconies and paths, wonder at its transparent walls, and marvel at its sheer size: **Biblioteca Vasconcelos,** in Mexico City, Mexico, covers a whopping 409,000 square feet (38,000 sq m).

8

FAIRY-TALE FEATURE

With its fancy high ceilings and super-ornate architecture, the library at Austria's **Admont Abbey monastery,** built in 1776, has been compared with the castle library from Disney's classic film *Beauty and the Beast.*

EIGHT

MONSTER FISH

CHECK OUT SOME OF THE MOST SIZABLE SWIMMERS LURKING IN OUR OCEANS, RIVERS, AND LAKES.

SHARKS PUSH THEIR STOMACH OUT OF THEIR MOUTH TO VOMIT.

2 OPEN WIDE!

Though it could swallow you whole with its five-foot (1.5-m)-wide mouth, the **whale shark** wouldn't want to. These docile filter feeders grow as big as a school bus on a diet of plankton and tiny fish, which they eat at a rate of three to six pounds (1.5 to 2.7 kg) an hour.

1 BIG NOSE KNOWS

The Mississippi River, U.S.A., watershed is home to seven-foot (2.1-m)-long **paddlefish**, sometimes called spoonies. They use electroreceptors on their long snouts—which are about a third as long as their total body length!—to locate food and to navigate their migration.

5 BIG BITE

Great white sharks, the biggest predatory fish on Earth, can grow to around 20 feet (6 m) long. But what makes these humongous hunters so successful isn't their size—it's their deadly bite, which scientists estimate can crush with about two tons (1.8 t) of force.

8 CARP DIEM!

In Southeast Asia, these nearly 10-foot (3-m)-long giant **Siamese carp** were once part of the local menu, but their numbers have dropped so quickly that they're now protected by local governments, including the Kingdom of Cambodia, where they're recognized as the national fish.

4 RIVER GIANTS

Our planet's biggest freshwater fish tops out at more than 10 feet (3 m) long and 650 pounds (294 kg). Once plentiful, the **Mekong giant catfish** is now facing extinction because of dams and overfishing in the Southeast Asian river where it lives.

YOU CAN TELL THE AGE OF A FISH FROM THE GROWTH RINGS IN ITS SCALES.

7 WHOLE LOTTA MOLA!

Found in temperate and tropical oceans worldwide, these round, bony beasts can grow up to 14 feet (4.3 m) tall, 10 feet (3 m) long, and nearly 5,000 pounds (2,268 kg)—as heavy as a minivan! Because they bask near the ocean's surface, **mola** are also known as sunfish.

3 READY FOR BATTLE

The salt water-dwelling **beluga sturgeon**, which is hunted and raised in aquaculture farms for its caviar, protects itself with thick armored plates and lives for more than 100 years. It reaches an adult size as long and as heavy as a 25-foot (7.6-m) camper trailer.

6 TREACHEROUS TAIL

In sandy, coastal waters of the Indo-Pacific, stingrays up to 10 feet (3 m) long hunt for fish and invertebrates and generally leave humans alone. But watch out! A **cowtail stingray** can bend its long tail up over its back and inflict serious damage with its venomous serrated spine.

1 TOUCH OF GLASS

If you like collecting sea glass—those colorful bits of broken glass tumbled smooth by ocean waves and sand—you'll love **broken glass mulch.** Dress up your garden using broken glass as a gravel, adding color, air, and light to the landscape.

EIGHT
RAD **RECYCLED** CREATIONS

HEY, DON'T THROW THAT AWAY! CHECK OUT THESE AWESOME WAYS TO TURN TRASH INTO TREASURE.

2 POP A WHEELIE

Tires are designed to be durable—which means if they end up in a landfill, they won't biodegrade (decompose) anytime soon. Fortunately, the bouncy black stuff can be chopped up or reused whole in numerous ways, like in a **used tire playground.**

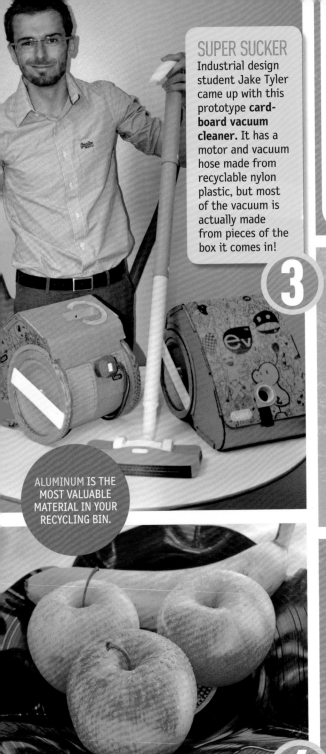

SUPER SUCKER

Industrial design student Jake Tyler came up with this prototype **cardboard vacuum cleaner**. It has a motor and vacuum hose made from recyclable nylon plastic, but most of the vacuum is actually made from pieces of the box it comes in!

3

ALUMINUM IS THE MOST VALUABLE MATERIAL IN YOUR RECYCLING BIN.

BRILLIANT BACKPACK

4

It's one thing to wash out and reuse a water bottle or sandwich bag; it's quite another to weave a once boring bottle into bright and durable fabric for **recycled plastic backpacks and purses.** This bodacious bag is made with 100 percent recycled polyester. Talk about fashion forward!

5

IN THE MIX

Chinese companies have taken 3-D printing to a new level, using wet concrete mixed with recycled glass and steel as their printing material. These **recycled concrete houses** are cheap for their size, and they go up quickly: One company printed 10 houses in less than a day!

7

JUST ROLL WITH IT

Riding a bicycle is one way to reduce your carbon footprint, but you can go even greener if you ride a **recycled aluminum bike** made from empty soda cans or scrap aluminum.

6

OLDIE BUT A GOODIE

This recycled bowl puts a new spin on serving food. It was made from the granddaddy of CDs and MP3s: the **vinyl record!** Now that's music to our ears.

CAFFEINATED COUTURE

Researchers have developed the technology to use recycled coffee grounds in creating environmentally friendly fabrics. **Coffee clothes** are light, odor-resistant, and already available through popular brands you'd see at the local mall or sporting goods store.

8

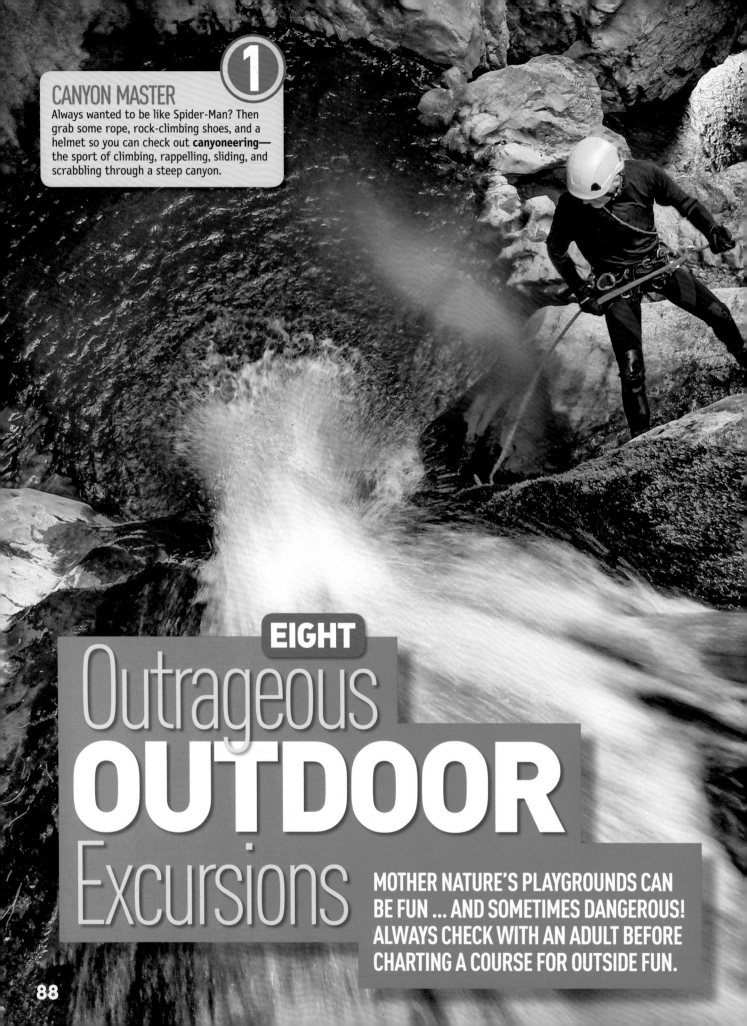

CANYON MASTER

1

Always wanted to be like Spider-Man? Then grab some rope, rock-climbing shoes, and a helmet so you can check out **canyoneering**—the sport of climbing, rappelling, sliding, and scrabbling through a steep canyon.

EIGHT
Outrageous
OUTDOOR
Excursions

MOTHER NATURE'S PLAYGROUNDS CAN BE FUN ... AND SOMETIMES DANGEROUS! ALWAYS CHECK WITH AN ADULT BEFORE CHARTING A COURSE FOR OUTSIDE FUN.

THE BIGGEST GAME OF TAG WAS PLAYED BY 2,202 STUDENTS IN INDIANA, U.S.A.

DOWN AND DIRTY

The parks department in Westland, Michigan, U.S.A., believes you shouldn't be afraid to **get dirty!** Kids are invited to bake mud pies, mud wrestle, mud soak, and get as messy as possible at its annual Mud Day event.

BALANCE BEAMS

Inspired by lumberjacks who once guided logs down rivers, **boom runs** are now popular at the annual Lumberjack World Championships, where competitors race and leap across a string of roly-poly logs to see who can make it down and back in the shortest amount of time.

SWING LIKE TARZAN

Get a good grip and away you go! If you can't find a banyan tree or a liana (jungle vine) in your neighborhood, any **rope tree swing** will do. Always make sure the tree is sturdy enough to support you and that you have a safe place to land!

RACE YOU TO THE TOP

Annual **tree-climbing competitions** are held across the world to test the skills of professional arborists and rescue workers. Race to the top and have a wild, towering good time!

SLIP 'N' SLIDE

At the end of a long hike, who doesn't want to take a dive into a swimming hole? This natural Arizona waterslide, known as **Slide Rock,** is so popular with the locals that they named the surrounding state park after it.

BLAZE A TRAIL

They call it **bouldering:** climbing up large rocks using only your hands and feet, with no ropes. All you need to get going is some loose chalk for a sweat-free grip and climbing shoes that wedge your toes where they need to go.

RIDE LIKE THE WIND

Wonder what it feels like to fly? For those who love an adrenaline rush, **paragliding** gives you the opportunity to find out! Gliders launch from a flat surface simply by letting the wind pick up their sail.

TURN THE PAGE FOR MORE OUTDOOR ADVENTURES!

WHERE IN THE WORLD?

EIGHT INCREDIBLE GEOCACHES ACROSS THE GLOBE

1 The Infinity Gauntlet, a comic-book-inspired, seven-step puzzle cache in Oregon, U.S.A.

2 Bananaaaa Nightclub Nachtcache, a fully-functioning "minion disco" in Wietze, Germany, that powers up between 6 p.m. and 2 a.m., local time

3 Mission Impossible, a multistep puzzle cache in North Wales, U.K., that finishes with a cable-lowered Tom Cruise doll, which has the cache strapped to its chest

4 Phantom of the Opera, a multistep cache in Oslo, Norway, that takes you to the rooftop of the opera house

BEFORE YOU ATTEMPT A GEOCACHE QUEST, BE SURE TO ALWAYS CHECK WITH AN ADULT!

Holding your instructions, you look closely from top to bottom at the tree in front of you. You examine it for anything weird attached to it, anything crafted to blend in but actually made from something else. Wait a second ... your instructions say to look underneath it, but how can you look under a tree rooted in the ground? You scan the area and spot a hollow log just to the side of it. Bingo! You check inside and find your treasure.

Can you guess what you are doing? It's geocaching, a worldwide game of hide-and-seek in which people conceal waterproof packages filled with treasures and post clues on websites so that others can find what they've stashed. **More than 2 million "geocaches" are hidden somewhere on Earth, with some on every continent—including Antarctica.** They're under rocks and bridges, inside caves and closets, stuck to doorways and street signs. They've even made their way beyond Earth's atmosphere ... to the International Space Station!

Some geocaches are containers as small as your finger, with just a sheet of paper rolled up inside on which those who find it can log their names. Others are large enough to hold a notebook, pencil, and "swag"—fun stuff you can show off in selfies or bring home as a souvenir of your successful expedition. It's customary to leave a note inside the logbook so others will know you discovered it. And if you take a piece of swag, be sure to leave something behind for the next person who opens the box.

Games like this first started during the 1800s in Europe, where they called it "letterboxing"; clues were handwritten or passed through word of mouth. Today, more than 10 million people are registered online to play at geocaching—most using smartphone apps and websites that show the location of different geocaches. Some of these are listed with direct GPS coordinates, but others use secret codes, puzzles, and riddles to reveal their location. "Earthcaches" are a special kind of geocache that highlight geology, leading people to beautiful sandbars or waterfalls, an exposed fossil in the side of a cliff, or folded rock that shows the effect of pressure deep inside the Earth.

Geocachers try to keep a low profile in public so their hunt won't be ruined by "muggles," the term they use for anyone who doesn't play the game. The most complex geocaches involve many steps and can take days to finally discover.

Happy treasure hunting!

5

Kuang Si Waterfalls, an Earthcache in Laos that takes you to an elaborate network of cascading waterfalls and terraced swimming pools

6

Mission 4: Southern Bowl, in São Paolo, Brazil, the only remaining swag-loaded geocache hidden by *Planet of the Apes* film promotion crews in 2001

7

Bridges and Arches of Central Park, in New York City, U.S.A., a 32-stage cache that traces hidden codes in the architecture of the park

8

Beatles Abbey Road, a virtual cache in London, U.K., that's monitored by webcam, allowing you and your friends to re-create the famous image of a Beatles album cover as you stroll across the street

KNITS THAT ARE THE BOMB!

WOOLLY STITCHES AREN'T JUST FOR GRANDMA. "YARN-BOMBERS" CAN MAKE ALMOST ANYTHING LOOK COZY IN A SWEATER.

2
SIT BACK AND LAUGH
To make sure that property owners wouldn't object and unravel all three miles (5 km) of yarn (and 30 hours of work!), Lorna and Jill Watt, sisters who knitted and crocheted this San Francisco, California, U.S.A., **park bench,** asked permission before they set it up.

1
FAIRY-TALE TREE
Artist Babukatorium was inspired to dress this tree in her native Veszprém, Hungary, in **rainbow crocheted spiderwebs** after seeing a performance of Shakespeare's play *A Midsummer Night's Dream.*

3
HATS OFF
A **humongous horizontal head** outside the library in Calne, England, got a colorful new topper courtesy of the Marden Belles Women's Institute. The sculpture's considerable cap took six months for the local group to create.

HAPPY FEET

4

Talk about putting your best foot forward! Yarn-bombers Lorna and Jill Watt's **mailbox monster feet** can turn a humdrum errand—like a run to the post office—into something a lot more fun.

TIME TO UPGRADE

5

Got any quarters? How about really big fingers? Lorna Watt repurposed a **pay phone** in San Mateo, California, U.S.A., by knitting a cover that turned it into a giant smartphone. Unfortunately, your call cannot be completed as dialed—the pay phone is broken!

STITCHING FOR A CAUSE

7

When volunteers dressed Pittsburgh, Pennsylvania, U.S.A.'s Andy Warhol Bridge in crochet, knit, and woven squares, it had nothing to do with chilly weather. This **"Knit the Bridge"** community-building campaign lasted about a month, and then the blankets were donated to local homeless shelters.

RESEARCH SHOWS THAT THE REPETITIVE MOTION OF KNITTING REDUCES STRESS AND HELPS WITH MEMORY.

CLIMB ABOARD

6

Texas artist Magda Sayeg sparked the yarn-bombing movement in 2005 when she knit a cover for a doorknob. One of her first large-scale installations was this **knitted bus** in Mexico City. Would this inspire you to hop on?

PRETTY MACHO

8

Artist Theresa Honeywell's pink knitted **"motorcycle cozy"** flips the stereotype of a biker clad in black leather right on its frilly pink head. This beautiful bike is ready to burn some rubber.

1

YOU ARE WHAT YOU EAT

Near the rocky shores of California, U.S.A., and Baja California, in Mexico, a neon **Spanish shawl nudibranch** *(Flabellina iodinea)* is hard to miss crawling on corals or fluttering through open water. This flashy finger-length slug gets its bright color by recycling pigments from its favorite food, tiny plantlike jellyfish known as hydroids.

EIGHT

GNARLY **NUDIBRANCHS**

THE NICKNAME "SEA SLUG" DOESN'T DO THESE MARVELOUS MOLLUSKS JUSTICE.

2

PATTERN PLAY

Fluorescent stripes and polka dots turn the **Nembrotha kubaryana's** costume into a can't-miss warning sign for potential predators. Distinguished by its often orange foot, this nudibranch lives in tropical western Pacific and Indian Ocean waters and grows up to 4.7 inches (12 cm) in length.

NUDIBRANCHS NAVIGATE USING **FACE** TENTACLES THAT CAN SMELL AND TASTE.

SUCH A SHOW-OFF

4 The beautiful plumes of *Cyerce nigricans* are coated with toxic mucus that tastes nasty to fish. The plumes also come off like a lizard's tail when this sea slug feels threatened, wriggling to distract predators while the bite-size nudibranch makes its getaway.

DANCE FOR THE FRILL OF IT

5 **Spanish dancer** nudibranchs (*Hexabranchus sanguineus*)—the largest member of the sea slug family—can be found swirling their skirts in the tropical waters of the western Pacific and Indian Oceans. They grow up to 18 inches (45 cm) long, crawling or swimming in search of tasty sea sponges.

DEADLY SURFER

3 The thumbnail-size **blue dragon** (*Glaucus atlanticus*) cruises tropical oceans, suspended on the surface by a stomach bubble while it searches for its favorite snack: Portuguese man-o-wars. Look, but don't touch! The dragon hides jellyfish poison it gets from its prey in the tips of its frilly blue fingers.

FUZZY FACE

6 ***Nembrotha cristata*** looks like he's ready for someone to scratch him behind his little black ears! Except those aren't actually ears: They're rhinophores (for smelling). The green moustache is really his tongue, and the little green wings are his stinging gills. On second thought, you shouldn't touch him ...

DRESSED FOR ACTION

7 If the University of California Santa Cruz, U.S.A., ever gets tired of its banana slug mascot, we suggest trading up with ***Chromodoris annae*** as a replacement. This finger-length sea slug already wears the university's blue and yellow colors, and when it comes to competition, stingers beat slime every time.

SPOTS, HORNS, AND WINGS

8 Its frilly pigtails, mustache, and daisy-shaped spots make ***Bornella anguilla*** look more like a cartoon character than like a pinkie-finger-length sea slug. This nudibranch, named for its eel-like way of swimming, lives in tropical waters of the Indian and western Pacific Oceans.

EIGHT STAIRCASES THAT INSPIRE

WHO WANTS TO TAKE THE ELEVATOR WHEN YOU HAVE STEPS LIKE THESE?

PICTURE PATH

2

A group of neighbors worked with city officials, professional tile masons, and mosaic artists to decorate the **16th Avenue steps** in San Francisco, California, U.S.A. Their work shows a sea-to-sky theme, flowing from marine scenes at the bottom to birds, leaves, and stars at the top.

STEP BACK IN TIME

1

Each wall of the ancient **Chand Baori** in India is criss-crossed with steps—about 3,500 in all—that once made it easy for people coming from all directions to quench their thirst in the well at the bottom.

GRAND ASCENT

3

Rumor has it that J. K. Rowling found some of her Harry Potter inspiration from the **Lello & Irmão Bookstore** in Porto, Portugal, which she often visited while she was an English teacher abroad. The stairs do seem to resemble those from Hogwarts, don't you think?

SWEET STAIRS

Architecture firm Tetrarc designed this colorful staircase with multicolor wood strips on its underside for the **School of Arts in Saint-Herblain, France.** From a distance, its twisty shape looks like stretched-out saltwater taffy!

LOOP THE LOOP

The **Tiger & Turtle Magic Mountain** stairs in Germany resemble a stomach-flipping roller coaster, but instead of speeding through those curves and twists you have to walk them step-by-step. Except for the loops, of course, which are closed off by barriers. That would be a dizzying descent!

THE LONGEST STAIRWAY IN THE WORLD IS IN SWITZERLAND AND HAS 11,674 STEPS.

WALKING IN CIRCLES

The **Umschreibung** steps in Munich, Germany—also called the "never-ending" or "endless" staircase—seem to change their shape depending on where you stand.

NATURE'S SPIRAL

Look at all familiar? That's because the tower staircases Antoni Gaudí designed for the **Basílica Sagrada Família** in Barcelona, Spain, reflect the Golden Ratio, a rule of measure that can also be found in the spiral of seashells, pinecones, sunflower seed heads, and DNA.

EVERY WHICH WAY

They might look like they're built from Popsicle sticks, but the 15 interlocking staircases that form **Endless Stair** were actually built from tulipwood for the 2013 London Design Festival. Step up, and up, and up to enjoy the view!

1

UNDER THE RAINBOW
It looks like a rainbow hot tub, but the **Grand Prismatic Spring** in Yellowstone National Park is actually a scalding pool of acid. Yikes! Its varying colors represent different habitats for bacteria that have mastered life in an extreme environment.

EIGHT

DANGERS OF NATURE

IF LOOKS COULD KILL ... SOMETIMES NATURE IS BEST ADMIRED FROM A DISTANCE.

WHEN TOXIC CREATURES USE BRIGHT COLORS TO WARN PREDATORS, IT'S CALLED APOSEMATISM.

2

FATAL FROGGIES
In tropical forests of Central and South America, touching **poison dart frogs** can put you in the hospital—or worse! Scientists believe these frogs become toxic as a result of eating ants, beetles, and termites that carry plant poisons.

BAD BLOSSOMS
You don't want these lacy white blooms in your wildflower bouquet! Sap from the **giant hogweed** causes human skin to blister just like a third-degree burn when exposed to sunlight.

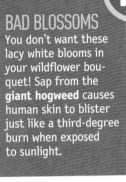

5

DEADLY BITE
Though the **boomslang** is highly venomous—one of the most venomous snakes in Africa— fewer than 10 human deaths have been recorded from their bites. It is a "rear-fanged" snake, meaning its fangs are way back in its mouth—requiring the reptile to open its mouth to nearly 180 degrees to take a big bite. Boomslangs enjoy a diet of frogs, lizards, chameleons, birds, and mice.

OOOH—BURN!

3

Fire corals get their name not from their shape or bright colors but from the pain they can inflict on people who happen to touch them. These corals are distant relatives of jellyfish and use the same stinging cells—nematocysts—to capture prey and ward off predators.

BLUE RINGS OF DEATH

7

The bottle-cap-size **blue ringed octopus** is as cute as a button, but watch out for this little guy: It uses its sharp beak and poisonous saliva to paralyze prey, as well as any humans who make the unfortunate mistake of picking it up near swimming beaches in Australia.

FORBIDDEN FRUIT

6

Those apples may look tasty, but stay away! All parts of the **manchineel tree** are poisonous, and ingesting any part of it can be deadly. Found in Florida, Mexico, Central America, and many Caribbean islands, the tree oozes a toxic sap that reportedly causes blisters when it touches the skin.

SERIOUS STINGER
Beneath what looks like a harmless iridescent bubble lies the **Portuguese man-of-war's** dangerous weapon: stinging tentacles that extend an average of 30 feet (10 m). They work like a dragline to stun krill and small fish—or an unfortunate swimmer's arm or leg. Watch where you swim!

8

FAR-OUT SHOTS

BIRD'S-EYE VIEWS SERVE UP A FRESH PERSPECTIVE ON THE BEAUTY OF OUR PLANET.

WHEELS AND WILDCATS
2

In Arabic it's known as the **Rujm el-Hiri,** or "stone heap of the wildcat"; in Hebrew, it's the **Gilgal Refaim,** or "wheel of giants." This tomb in Israel dates back nearly 5,000 years and was built from 40,000 tons (36,287 t) of crumbled stone.

GO WITH THE FLOW
1

Rice fields in China make the whole landscape seem as if it's flowing downhill and swirling around trees. But the fields are actually flat, narrow platforms stacked around the curve of hills to capture rain and prevent erosion.

TREE OF LIFE
3

Don't feel sorry for this lone **acacia tree.** Hundreds of paths leading to it show that the animals of Tsavo East National Park in Kenya are keeping it company, traveling for miles through the arid savanna to seek shelter in its shade.

THE COLONY

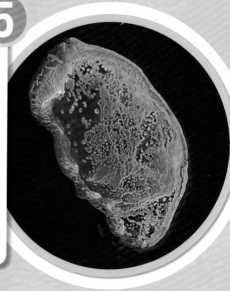

It may look like a blue blob from above, but **Arrecife Alacranes**, the largest reef in the Gulf of Mexico, is actually teeming with life near the surface: corals, fish, and sea turtles, as well as seabirds, insects, and a handful of humans who occupy one of the reef's five tiny islands.

5

4

DRAWING IN THE SAND

They might look like doodles, but scientists think **Nasca lines** in the desert of southern Peru were actually ancient ritualistic paths that locals walked while praying for water. The lines were built by moving dark stones to the edges of the path, exposing the lighter ground of the valley floor.

BIG BUSINESS

You know it washes up on beaches, but did you know that seaweed is also used in salty snacks, sushi rolls, and sausages? **Seaweed farms** satisfy the growing appetite for these edible algae, floating their crop on ropes to catch maximum sunlight.

7

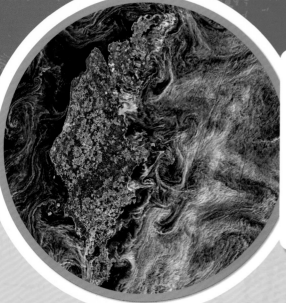

6

WONDERFUL WATERCOLORS

When seasonal currents churn up food from the bottom of the ocean, microscopic phytoplankton really shine. They produce bright green **algae blooms** like these, photographed by a NASA satellite.

SATELLITES CAN SPOT OBJECTS ON EARTH AS SMALL AS A BACKPACK.

8

DYNAMIC DELTA

The vast expanse of the Okavango Delta, in Botswana, features permanent **marshlands and plains** that flood seasonally. Some of the world's most endangered mammals—including the African wild dog and the black rhinoceros—call the delta home.

① DRESSED FOR THE OCCASION

When the **brown mimic octopus** dons black and white stripes and hides six of its arms in a hole, even a true poisonous sea snake could be fooled by the resemblance. This crafty cephalopod can also mimic a lionfish or a poisonous sole, depending on which predator it wants to avoid.

THIS AMAZING OCTOPUS CAN "MIMIC" UP TO 15 DIFFERENT SPECIES!

EIGHT

TRICKY MIMICS

IT'S A CASE OF MISTAKEN IDENTITY ... BUT THAT'S EXACTLY HOW THESE DECEPTIVE DUPLICATES SURVIVE.

② TOO PRETTY TO EAT

The Malaysian **orchid mantis** isn't trying to hide from predators; it looks like a flower because it *is* the predator. And the disguise is so good that this insect can catch its dinner even without a real orchid nearby.

DOGS TRY TO MIMIC THE HAND MOVEMENTS OF PEOPLE WITH THEIR PAWS.

CREEPY CRAWLY

4 With spots that look like eyes and an inflatable tail, **snake-mimic caterpillars** pull off a striking impersonation of the most fearsome slithering creatures on the planet. Some caterpillars have even added a forked "tongue." Now that's creepy!

SIMIAN SIMILARITY

3 The **monkey orchid** definitely resembles the golden lion tamarin monkey, but mimicking the mammal doesn't help it lure pollinators. Instead, the flower draws pollinating ants with its mushroom-like smell. The cute monkey face is just a bonus.

WHOOOO GOES THERE?

5 Maybe it's the eyeball-like pattern on its wings, or maybe it's because bold markings are generally a sign of danger. Whatever the case, one "look" from the **owl butterfly's** wings can cause a hungry songbird to throw on its air brakes and fly for cover from its pretend predator.

ALL IN THE DETAILS

7 How would you describe a dried-up leaf? Brown, twisted, bits broken off the edge from decay? The **Satanic leaf-tailed gecko** clearly had the same idea. You can even make out the pattern of stem and ribs visible on its skin!

DON'T MOVE A MUSCLE

6 An expert at camouflage, the Australian **tawny frogmouth** follows a simple strategy when scared: The bird hunkers down, shuts its eyes, and pulls off the best impersonation of a broken acacia tree branch you've ever seen.

HALF AND HALF

8 Is it a wasp? Maybe a praying mantis? Good guess, but the **wasp mantidfly** is actually in a completely different insect family. It doesn't carry a stinger and it doesn't bite humans, though it can use those front claws to grab other tasty bugs for its dinner.

BIG OL' HOLES

PEER IN TO CATCH A GLIMPSE OF EARTH'S DEEPEST, DARKEST SECRETS.

SWALLOWED HOLE

2

The 1,638-foot (499-m)-deep **Cave of Swallows** (El Sotano de las Golondrinas) in Mexico is popular with spelunkers and BASE jumpers. Named for the birds that fly overhead, this cave sports temps so cool near its bottom that clouds actually form inside of it.

DEEP BLUE

1

If you plopped a hollow mountain over the top of a 65-foot (20-m)-deep swimming hole, you'd have something like Utah, U.S.A.'s **Homestead Crater**, a natural, covered hot spring that makes scuba diving and swimming cozy in any season.

UNDERGROUND ADVENTURES

3

Mamet Cave (Jama Mamet) in Croatia is 656 feet (200 m) deep—roomy enough to have housed the world's first underground hot air balloon ride in 2014. The cave is shaped like an upside-down funnel, 197 feet (60 m) across at the top and opening wider the lower it gets.

THE STUDY
OF CAVES
IS CALLED
SPELEOLOGY.

4

BLOWOUT BELOW!

In 2014, scientists discovered several **huge Siberian craters** that they believe were caused by climate change. Methane deposits as big as Olympic-size swimming pools were trapped below the permafrost but were then released in a sudden, fantastic explosion that no one was around to hear. Kaboom!

5

NEW JOB FOR AN OLD HOLE

For more than a century, miners excavated South Dakota, U.S.A.'s **Homestake Mine** to pull gold and silver out of the ground. But today, physicists are using those deep, quiet chambers—some as far down as 8,000 feet (2,438 m) —to search for something completely different: dark matter, the invisible but massive stuff that fills more than a quarter of our universe!

6

HEAVEN BELOW EARTH

A popular tourist attraction in central Vietnam, **Paradise Cave** extends 19 miles (31 km) belowground with cathedral-like caverns, sparkling stalactites (ceiling spikes), and an underground river.

SATELLITES CAN
SPOT CRATERS
TOO BIG TO SEE
ON EARTH'S
SURFACE.

7

ONE FOR THE RECORDS

The year 1815 was unusually chilly. Why? Because that's when the biggest volcanic eruption in recorded history shaded Earth's atmosphere with ash, leaving behind the 3.7-mile (6-km)-wide and 3,609-feet (1,100-m)-deep **Mount Tambora Caldera** in Indonesia.

8

WATER DAMAGE

Sinkholes are usually caused by underground streams that dissolve rock, but geologists suspect the infamous **Guatemala City sinkhole** of 2010, which created a gaping chasm deep enough to swallow a three-story building, happened because of leaky pipes beneath the city.

HAIR-RAISING HAIRDOS

TALK ABOUT CRAZY COIFS! CHECK OUT SOME OF HISTORY'S MOST MARVELOUS MANES.

1

SPIKE IT

A style that dates back thousands of years, the **mohawk** was popularized in modern times by British punk bands in the '80s. Today, people use glue, egg whites, or plenty of hair gel to achieve this spiky do.

2

SHOW OFF

At **fantasy hair shows,** the bigger and bolder the style, the better. From pops of color to behemoth buns to manes molded into works of abstract art, models display hair that dares to be different.

MARIE ANTOINETTE'S HAIR SOMETIMES HID VASES FULL OF WATER TO KEEP THE FLOWERS FRESH.

3 THE MANE EVENT

Supported with wire scaffolding, Marie Antoinette's **gravity-defying do** towered more than three feet (0.9 m) tall. The infamous queen's coif was capped with flowers, feathers, and jewels—and was once even molded into the shape of an 18th-century battleship.

4 HELMET HAIR

In the 10th century, **Vikings** took great care of their hair, crafting combs out of animal antlers and even lightening their locks with ash. Shoulder-length hair—a sign of stature—was often fashioned into braids, which would spill out from the Vikings' helmets.

5 MAD SCIENCE

Physicist Albert Einstein may be remembered for his brilliance, but his **wild white hair** has also gone down in history. While his theory of relativity got plenty of notice, his unkempt mane and bushy mustache made him stand out even more.

6 BOLD BEARDS

These beards are anything but basic. The **"mermen"** trend—a look sparked from musical festivals around the world—has men rocking facial hair in bold hues resembling the manes of mythical mermaids.

7 BEE-UTIFUL

Women in the 1960s were buzzing about the **beehive do,** named because of its resemblance to the bug's abode. Another nickname for this retro style? The B-52, a nod to how its shape mirrors the nose of the airplane of the same name.

8 SUMO STYLE

Sumo wrestlers sport hair similar to what Japanese samurai warriors wore nearly 1,000 years ago. Slicked down with water and a special oil, the style stays put while the *rikishi* wrestle.

WILD WATERCRAFTS

HEADS UP, AQUANAUTS! THESE IMPRESSIVE VESSELS OFFER SUPERCOOL WAYS TO RIDE THE TIDE!

BOATS FLOAT HIGHER IN COLD, SALTY WATER THAN THEY DO IN WARM, FRESHWATER.

2 LEAPIN' LIFEBOAT

It rolls, it submerges five feet (1.5 m), and it breaches the surface at 40 miles an hour (64 km/h), imitating a frisky porpoise! Each **Seabreacher** recreational watercraft is custom designed to suit your style. But save your pennies—these (seal) puppies will set you back $80,000 to $100,000!

1 RIDE THE JETS

Like a water-powered jet-pack for your feet, the **Flyboard** shoots water out of boots (with the help of a Jet Ski or other jet-propelled miniboat) and sends the wearer up, over, around—even underwater!

5 FLYING ON WATER

Metal wings (or hydrofoils) protrude from underneath **Moth Class ultralight sailboats** and lift them above the waves, reducing their drag and allowing the small vessels to whip past other boats at speeds of more than 30 miles an hour (48 km/h).

8 WAVE-PIERCER

After zipping around the globe in 2008 and breaking world records, the **biodiesel-powered** *Earthrace* got a new name (*Ady Gil*), special-ops gear, and a new job: protecting marine species like whales from poachers. Though the vessel's work was cut short by a collision near Antarctica, architects are planning for an *Earthrace II* to continue her mission.

4 SMOOTH SAILING

For a relaxing day on or under the water, this might be just the ticket. Moving at a leisurely pace, the **EGO compact semi-submarine** offers passengers deck space for a picnic and an underwater cabin with panoramic windows to see the life aquatic without getting wet.

7 HOLD ON TIGHT!

With a strong wind, a harness strapped to their chest, and a board strapped to their feet, **kiteboarders** fly over the water at speeds up to 20 miles an hour (32 km/h). And when tilted just so, the kite can also pull riders as much as 50 feet (15 m) in the air, giving them some serious hang time above the waves.

3 MARINE MULTITASKER

The **Marion Hyper-Sub** combines the agility of a speedboat with the stealth of a submarine. Large chambers inside fill with water or air to change the buoyancy of the craft, allowing it to dive up to 1,200 feet (365 m) and achieve speeds of 35 miles an hour (56 km/h) on the surface.

6 ONE FOR THE TEAM

Once a sport of Hawaiian royalty, **outrigger canoe surfing** has made a comeback. Teams of four paddle out from shore to catch incoming waves and then turn around and ride them back!

INDEX

Boldface indicates illustrations.

PHOTO CREDITS

Cover (UP LE), Inge Johnsson/Alamy Stock Photo; Simon Bruty/Sports Illustrated/Getty Images; (CTR), Mattias Klum/National Geographic Creative; (LO LE), Eric Isselee/Shutterstock; (LO RT), Caters News Agency; 1 (Background), Eric Isselee/Shutterstock; 2-3 (Background), Michel & Gabrielle Therin-Weise/Alamy Stock Photo; 4 (UP), Steve Casino; 4 (CTR LE), frans lemmens/Alamy Stock Photo; 4 (CTR RT), Jurgen Otto/Solent News/Rex/Shutterstock; 4 (LO LE), Thomas Marent/ardea.com; 4 (LO RT), Todd Maisel/NY Daily News/Getty Images; 6 (1), Chris Maddaloni/Roll Call/Getty Images; 6 (2), Salavat Fidai; 6 (3), Splash News/Newscom; 7 (4), Solent News/Splash News/Newscom; 7 (5), Images Etc Ltd/Getty Images; 7 (6), Wang jiankang/Imaginechina/AP Photo; 7 (7), f11photo/Shutterstock; 7 (8), Warren Elsmore - artist in LEGO bricks. Photography by Michael Wolchover; 8 (1), Sandy Huffaker/Getty Images; 8 (2), Timothy A. Clary/AFP/Getty Images; 9 (3), Robyn Beck/AFP/Getty Images; 9 (4-6), Timothy A. Clary/AFP/Getty Images; 9 (7), John Vizcaino/Reuters; 9 (8), Bullit Marquez/AP Photo; 10 (1), Atlantide Phototravel/Corbis; 11 (2), Andrea Willmore/Shutterstock; 11 (3), Gudkov Andrey/Shutterstock; 11 (4), Przemyslaw Skibinski/Shutterstock; 11 (5), Cultura/Rex/Shutterstock; 11 (6), Carsten Peter/National Geographic Creative; 11 (7), Blaine Harrington III/Alamy Stock Photo; 11 (8), Eric Isselee/Shutterstock; 12 (Background), Juan Carlos Munoz/NPL/Minden Pictures; 12 (1), Benjamin Lowy/Getty Images; 12 (2), Colin Harris/era-images/Alamy Stock Photo; 12 (3), idreamipursue/Shutterstock; 12 (4), Micah Youello/Getty Images; 13 (Background), Owen Newman/NPL/Minden Pictures; 13 (5), Nikolay Vinokurov/Alamy Stock Photo; 13 (6), Eric Bouvet/Gamma-Rapho/Getty Images; 13 (7), Peter Wey/Alamy Stock Photo; 13 (8), Planet Observer/Getty Images; 14 (1), Steve Casino; 14 (2), Hong Yi; 15 (3), Michelle Reader; 15 (4), Jason Mecier; 15 (5), Kayleigh O'Connor/Solent News/AP Photo; 15 (6), CB2/ZOB/Supplied by Wenn/Newscom; 15 (7), Caters News Agency; 15 (8), Howard Davies/Alamy Stock Photo; 16 (1), Jenny Goodall/Daily Mail/Rex/Shutterstock; 16 (2), Pooch Selfie/Caters News Agency; 16 (3), Mercury Press and Media/Caters News Agency; 17 (4), Toru Hanai/Reuters; 17 (5), Vermont Novelty Toasters/Sol/Rex/AP Photo; 17 (6), Natsuki Sakai/Newscom; 17 (7), sevenke/Shutterstock; 17 (8), Melissakitchow.com/Sipa USA/Newscom; 18 (1), Martin Bernetti/AFP/Getty Images; 18 (2), Finnbarr Webster/Alamy Stock Photo; 19 (3), dislentev/Getty Images; 19 (4), Ronen Zvulun/Reuters; 19 (5), Thomas Nebbia/National Geographic Creative; 19 (5 Inset), Helen Sessions/Alamy Stock Photo; 19 (6), BPTU/Shutterstock; 19 (7), Dupont Underground/Hunt Laudi Studio; 19 (7 Inset), Dupont Underground/Pat Padua; 19 (8 & 8 Inset), Philip Scalia/Alamy Stock Photo; 20 (1), Will Oliver/AFP/Getty Images; 20 (2), Wenn/Alamy Stock Photo; 20 (3), Yoshikazu Tsuno/AFP/Getty Images; 21 (4), Nick Gammon/Alamy Stock Photo; 21 (5), Nils Jorgensen/Rex/Shutterstock; 21 (6), Greg Ryan/Alamy Stock Photo; 21 (7), Courtesy of RS Components; 21 (8), Funair; 22 (1), Justin Hobson/Shutterstock; 23 (2), NASA/SDO/AIA; 23 (3), CJ Gunther/EPA/Newscom; 23 (4), Mike Lyvers/Getty Images; 23 (5), Koichi Kamoshida/Jana Press/Zumapress; 23 (6), RelexFoto.de/Getty Images; 23 (7), Marco Simoni/robertharding/Getty Images; 23 (8), David Tipling Photo Library/Alamy Stock Photo; 24-25 (Background), ESA/NASA; 25 (1), Eric Baccega/naturepl.com; 25 (2), Vinicius Tupinamba/Shutterstock; 25 (3), Thomas Marent/Minden Pictures/Getty Images; 25 (4), Raphaela Tesch/Alamy Stock Photo; 25 (5), Eva-Lotta Jansson/Bloomberg/Getty Images; 25 (6), epa european pressphoto agency b.v./Alamy Stock Photo; 25 (7), Jason Reed/Getty Images; 25 (8), imagebroker/Alamy Stock Photo; 26 (1), Alamo Drafthouse/Caters News Agency; 26 (2), Dubravko Grakalic/Alamy Stock Photo; 26 (3), LOOK Die Bildagentur der Fotografen GmbH/Alamy Stock Photo; 27 (4), WR Publishing/Alamy Stock Photo; 27 (5), Hot Tub Cinema/Caters News Agency; 27 (6), Kika Press/Zumapress/Newscom; 27 (7), Suzanne Long/Alamy Stock Photo; 27 (8 & 8 Inset), Christopher Nicholson/Alamy Stock Photo; 28 (1), Tribune Content Agency LLC/Alamy Stock Photo; 28 (2), Ronald Martinez/Getty Images; 29 (3), Brett Hansbauer/Sports Illustrated/Getty Images; 29 (4), PCN Photography/Alamy Stock Photo; 29 (5), Jerome Levitch/Corbis; 29 (6), Leo Mason sports photos/Alamy Stock Photo; 29 (7), Ian MacNicol/Getty Images; 29 (8), AP Photo; 30 (1), kevinhung/Shutterstock; 31 (2), Antonio Pisacreta/Ropi/Zumapress/Newscom; 31 (3), David Wall Photo/Getty Images; 31 (4), The Asahi Shimbun/Getty Images; 31 (5), Walter Bibikow Danita Delimont Photography/Newscom; 31 (6), Svetlana Yudina/Shutterstock; 31 (7), Janis Maleckis/Shutterstock; 31 (8), Gerd Ludwig/National Geographic Creative; 32-33 (Background), David Trood/Getty Images; 32 (1), Nate Jenkins/AP Photo; 32 (3), Mel Melcon/Los Angeles Times/Getty Images; 33 (5), Patti McConville/Alamy Stock Photo; 33 (8), John Elk/Getty Images; 34 (1), Bildagentur Geduldig/Alamy Stock Photo; 34 (2), Laszlo Lewis/Getty Images; 35 (3), M. Sobreira/Alamy Stock Photo; 35 (4), Danita Delimont/Alamy Stock Photo; 35 (5), Ian Cumming/Zumapress/Newscom; 35 (6), Sue Cunningham Photographic/Alamy Stock Photo; 35 (7), Gardel Bertrand/Getty Images; 35 (8), ArtyAlison/Getty Images; 36 (1), Courtesy of Kayla Kromer. Photo by Heather Leah Kennedy; 36 (2), Richard Wayman/Stockimo/Alamy Stock Photo; 37 (3), Courtesy of it design; 37 (4), Rex Features/AP Photo; 37 (5), OGE Creative Group; 37 (6), Animi Causa; 37 (7), Anita Bowen; 37 (8), Montserrat T Diez/Corbis; 38 (1), Peter Macdiarmid/Getty Images; 38 (2), Alexey Senin/Alamy Stock Photo; 38 (3), Allan Baxter/Getty Images; 39 (4), imagebroker/Alamy Stock Photo; 39 (5), Christian Wilkinson/Shutterstock; 39 (6), MJ Photography/Alamy Stock Photo; 39 (7), Courtesy of Joana Vasconcelos. Photo: Nacho Doce/Reuters; 39 (8), Paul Rushton/Alamy Stock Photo; 40 (1), Richard Levine/Alamy Stock Photo; 40 (2), Chuck Eckert/Alamy Stock Photo; 41 (3), T photography/Shutterstock; 41 (4), Brooks Kraft/Corbis; 41 (5), Niels Poulsen DK/Alamy Stock Photo; 41 (6), Directphoto Collection/Alamy Stock Photo; 41 (7), Rafael Ramirez Lee/Shutterstock; 41 (8), Tanteckken/Dreamstime.com; 42 (1), frans lemmens/Alamy Stock Photo; 42 (2), Kevin Zaouali/Caters News Agency; 42 (3), imagebroker/Alamy Stock Photo; 43 (4), blickwinkel/Alamy Stock Photo; 43 (5), AsianDream/Getty Images; 43 (6), Tao Ming Xinhua News Agency/Newscom; 43 (7), The Asahi Shimbun/Getty Images; 43 (8), Debra James/Shutterstock; 44 (1), Trevor Watchous/Eye Em/Getty Images; 45 (2), Reinhard Dirscherl/Getty Images; 45 (3), Tui De Roy/naturepl.com; 45 (4), Cyril Ruoso/naturepl.com; 45 (5), Kerryn Parkinson/Norfanz/Zumapress/Newscom; 45 (6), National Geographic Creative/Alamy Stock Photo; 45 (7), Geoff Smith/Alamy Stock Photo; 45 (8), Rex/Shutterstock; 46-47 (Background), Cyril Ruoso/Minden Pictures; 46 (1), Rob Cousins/Alamy Stock Photo; 46 (2), vario images GmbH & Co.KG/Alamy Stock Photo; 46 (3), agefotostock/Alamy Stock Photo; 46 (4), Norbert Wu/Minden Pictures/Getty Images; 47 (5), Nature Picture Library/Alamy Stock Photo; 47 (6), petographer/Alamy Stock Photo; 47 (7), Dickie Duckett/FLPA/Minden Pictures; 47 (8), blickwinkel/Alamy Stock Photo; 47 (UP LE), FLPA/Alamy Stock Photo; 47 (UP RT), Pat Morris/ardea.com; 47 (CTR), imagebroker/Alamy Stock Photo; 48 (1), Courtesy of Albatros Adventure Marathon; 48 (2), Mike King/LNP/Rex/Shutterstock; 49 (3), Andrew Lloyd/Alamy Stock Photo; 49 (4), Aled Llywelyn/Zumapress/Newscom; 49 (5), Chiang Ying-ying/AP Photo; 49 (6), Eric Friedman; 49 (7), Clifford Hill; 49 (8), Emma Wood/Alamy Stock Photo; 50 (1), Courtesy of Cipriano Custom Pools; 50 (2), Graham Monro/gm photographics/Getty Images; 51 (3), Courtesy of James Law Cybertecture International; 51 (4), VCG/Getty Images; 51 (5), Marc Gerritsen/Sheltered Images/Newscom; 51 (6), Danita Delimont/Alamy Stock Photo; 51 (7), Blend Images/Alamy Stock Photo; 51 (8), robertharding/Alamy Stock Photo; 52 (1), Stephen J. Boitano/LightRocket/Getty Images; 52 (2), Courtesy of Beachy Media; 52 (3), Kobi Levi; 53 (4), Courtesy of Greats Brand; 53 (5), Jean-Marc David/Sipa/Newscom; 53 (6), Europics/Newscom; 53 (7), Britta Pedersen/EPA/Newscom; 53 (8), Silvia Fado; 54 (1), Jurgen Otto; 54 (2), Nicky Bay Photography; 55 (3), James Carmichael Jr/NHPA/Photoshot/Newscom; 55 (4), Piotr Naskrecki/Minden Pictures; 55 (5-6, 8), Nicky Bay Photography; 55 (7), Jurgen Otto; 56 (1), Steve Gschmeissner/Science Source; 56 (2), Power and Syred/Science Source; 56 (3), Science Picture Co/Science Source; 57 (4), Cultura RM Exclusive/Gregory S. Paulson/Getty Images; 57 (5), Laszlo Podor/Getty Images; 57 (6), TothGaborGyula/Getty Images; 57 (7), Alex Hyde/NPL/Minden Pictures; 57 (8), Iain Lawrie/Getty Images; 58 (1), Paul Nicklen/National Geographic Creative; 58 (2), Artiga Photo/Getty Images; 59 (3), Amy Davis/Baltimore Sun/MCT/Getty Images; 59 (4), Steve Russell/Toronto Star/Getty Images; 59 (5), Matej Kastelic/Shutterstock; 59 (6), Asia Sports Ventures/Action Images/Reuters; 59 (7), Rene Johnston/Toronto Star/Getty Images; 59 (8), Ben Franke/Alamy Stock Photo; 60 (1), Stephen Barnes/Europe/Alamy Stock Photo; 61 (2), Milosz Maslanka/Shutterstock; 61 (3), Auscape/UIG/Getty Images; 61 (4), Aflo Co. Ltd./Alamy Stock Photo; 61 (5), Courtesy of Agile LeVin/Visit Turks and Caicos Islands; 61 (6), nick baylis/Alamy Stock Photo; 61 (7), Virginian-Pilot, Drew C. Wilson/AP Photo; 61 (8), 141crew/Shutterstock; 62 (Background), Patrick Aventurier/Getty Images; 63 (1), Sebastiano Tusa; 63 (4), Hulton Archive/Getty Images; 63 (5), Louisa Gouliamaki/Getty Images; 63 (6), DeAgostini/Getty Images; 63 (8), Dave J Hogan/Getty Images; 63 (LO RT), Boris Horvat/AFP/Getty Images; 63 (LO LE), Patrick Aventurier/Sipa/Newscom; 64 (1), Ahmad Faizal Yahya/Shutterstock; 64 (2), keith taylor/Alamy Stock Photo; 64 (3), Anders Blomqvist/Getty Images; 65 (4), Akihiro Sugimoto/Aflo/Newscom; 65 (5), rollercoaster.rs (6), David R. Frazier Photolibrary, Inc./Alamy Stock Photo; 65 (7), Caters News Agency; 65 (8), JTB Photo/UIG/Getty Images; 66 (1), Michael & Patricia Fogden/Minden Pictures; 66 (2), image-broker/Alamy Stock Photo; 67 (3), Sandesh Kadur/naturepl.com; 67 (4), Jim Zuckerman/Jaynes Gallery/ardea.com; 67 (5), Premaphotos/Alamy Stock Photo; 67 (6), Anthony Bannister/NHPA/Photoshot/Newscom; 67 (7), Tiago Queiroz/Agencia Estado/AP Photo; 67 (8), Thomas Marent/Visuals Unlimited/Corbis; 68 (1), Caters News Agency; 68 (2), Frederic Reglain/Gamma-Rapho/Getty Images; 69 (3), Robert J. Lang; 69 (4), Shaul Schwarz/Getty Images; 69 (5), Eric Vigier; 69 (6), Randy Duchaine/Alamy Stock Photo; 69 (7), Eric Gjerde; 69 (8), Robert J. Lang; 70 (1), Xinhua/Alamy Stock Photo; 70 (2), David Maxwell/Getty Images; 70 (3), Pete Saloutos/Getty Images; 71 (4), Mark Edward Harris/Getty Images; 71 (5), STR/AFP/Getty Images; 71 (6), Gaspa/ullstein bild/Getty Images; 71 (7), High Level Photography Ltd/Rex/AP Photo; 71 (8), Austral Int./Rex/AP Photo; 72 (1), Courtesy Craig S. Thomson; 72 (2), paul prescott/Alamy Stock Photo; 73 (3), Splash/Tomas Manina/Corbis; 73 (4), Mark Kolbe/Getty Images; 73 (5), Courtesy Cal-Earth Institute. Structure built by Alejandro Lopezy; 73 (6), urosr/Getty Images; 73 (7), Cyrille Gibot/Alamy Stock Photo; 73 (8), Olivier Morin/AFP/Getty Images; 74 (1), Ben Stansall/AFP/Getty Images; 75 (2), Hugh Threlfall/Alamy Stock Photo; 75 (3), CB2/ZOB/Wenn/Newscom; 75 (4), Mario Anzuoni/Reuters; 75 (5), Xinhua/Photoshot; 75 (6), I-Images/Zumapress/Newscom; 75 (7), Ishara S. Kodikara/AFP/Getty Images; 75 (8), Salvatore Di Nolfi/Keystone/AP Photo; 76-77 (Background), Carl Court/Hatton Garden Properties Ltd/Getty Images; 78 (1), Timothy A. Clary/AFP/Getty Images; 78 (2), Horizons WWP/TRVL/Alamy Stock Photo; 78 (3), Jaeyoun Kim (Iowa State University); 79 (4), Chip Somodevilla/Getty Images; 79 (5), Courtesy of Guardbot, Inc.; 79 (6), Nicolas Datiche/Sipa/Newscom; 79 (7), Robugtix Ltd.; 79 (8), David Mareuil/Anadolu Agency/Getty Images; 80 (1), Pierre Roussel/Newscom; 80 (2), Denis Budkov/Caters News Agency; 81 (3), All Canada Photos/Alamy Stock Photo; 81 (4), Sorin Papuc/Alamy Stock Photo; 81 (5), Caters News/Zumapress/Newscom; 81 (6), John Thys/AFP/Getty Images; 81 (7), Helen H. Richardson/Getty Images; 81 (8), robertharding/Alamy Stock Photo; 82 (1), Nancy Hoyt Belcher/Alamy Stock Photo; 82 (2), Nikreates/Alamy Stock Photo; 82 (3), Clarence Holmes Photography/Alamy Stock Photo; 83 (4), View Pictures Ltd/Alamy Stock Photo; 83 (5), Hot Spot Media; 83 (6), Irich Baumgarten/Getty Images; 83 (7), View Pictures Ltd/Alamy Stock Photo; 83 (8), Imagno/Getty Images; 84 (1), Mark Conlin/Alamy Stock Photo; 84 (2), Reinhard Dirscherl/ullstein bild/Getty Images; 85 (3), Leonid Serebrennikov/Alamy Stock Photo; 85 (4), Roland Seitre/naturepl.com; 85 (5), Daniel Badia/Caters News Agency; 85 (6), Andrey Nekrasov/Alamy Stock Photo; 85 (7), Stephen Frink Collection/Alamy Stock Photo; 85 (8), Zeb Hogan; 86 (1), imagebroker/Alamy Stock Photo; 86 (2), Andia/Photoshot; 87 (3), Caters News Agency. Used with permission of Jake Tyler; 87 (4), Courtesy of Patagonia; 87 (5), VCG/Getty Images; 87 (6), Zoonar GmbH/Alamy Stock Photo; 87 (7), Courtesy of ReCycle Cycles LLC; 87 (8), xPacifica/The Image Works; 88 (1), Predrag Vuckovic/Getty Images; 89 (2), Bill Pugliano/Getty Images; 89 (3), Eric Miller/Reuters; 89 (4), Colin McConnell/Toronto Star/Getty Images; 89 (5), imagebroker/Alamy Stock Photo; 89 (6), Universal Images Group/Getty Images; 89 (7), Andrew Kornylak/Akorn Photo LLC; 89 (8), Robb Kendrick/National Geographic Creative; 90-91 (Background), Tonello photography/Alamy Stock Photo; 90 (1), Daniel Borzynski/Alamy Stock Photo; 90 (2), Universal Pictures/Courtesy Everett Collection; 90 (3), AF archive/Alamy Stock Photo; 90 (4), Marco Cristofori/Getty Images; 91 (5), Jonas Gratzer/LightRocket/Getty Images; 91 (6), Kevin Schafer/Getty Images; 91 (7), Patrick Batchelder/Alamy Stock Photo; 91 (8), Martin Norris Travel Photography/Alamy Stock Photo; 92 (1), Babukatorium/Solent News/Rex Features/AP Photo; 92 (2), Lorna and Jill Watt, Knits for Life; 92 (3), Geoffrey Swaine/Rex/AP Photo; 93 (4-5), Lorna and Jill Watt, Knits for Life; 93 (6), Bournemouth News/Rex/Shutterstock; 93 (7), Gene J. Puskar/AP Photo; 93 (8), Rex/Shutterstock; 94 (1), Mauricio Handler/National Geographic Creative; 94 (2), Daniela Dirscherl/Getty Images; 95 (3), Andrew G Wood/Getty Images; 95 (4), Valerie & Ron Taylor/ardea.com; 95 (5), David Doubilet/National Geographic Creative; 95 (6), Doug Perrine/Getty Images; 95 (7), Terry Moore/Stocktrek Images/Getty Images; 95 (8), WaterFrame/Alamy Stock Photo; 96 (1), dbimages/Alamy Stock Photo; 96 (2), Connie J. Spinardi/Getty Images; 96 (3), Endless Travel/Alamy Stock Photo; 97 (4), Stephane Chalmeau; 97 (5-6), imagebroker/Alamy Stock Photo; 97 (7), rosmi duaso/Alamy Stock Photo; 97 (8), Guy Bell/Alamy Stock Photo; 98 (1), Tom Murphy/National Geographic Creative; 98 (2), Thomas Marent/Minden Pictures; 99 (3), Rainer von Brandis/Getty Images; 99 (4), Arterra Picture Library/Alamy Stock Photo; 99 (5), Mattias Klum/National Geographic Creative; 99 (6), Stefano Paterna/Alamy Stock Photo; 99 (7), Dray van Beeck/NiS/Minden Pictures; 99 (8), Stephen Frink Collection/Alamy Stock Photo; 100 (1), Jialiang Gao/Getty Images; 100 (2), Duby Tal/Albatross/Alamy Stock Photo; 100 (3), Yann Arthus-Bertrand/Getty Images; 101 (4), Martin Bernetti/AFP/Getty Images; 101 (5), NASA/Sipa/Newscom; 101 (6), USGS/NASA/Landsat 7; 101 (7), The Asahi Shimbun/Getty Images; 101 (8), Christophe Courteau/naturepl.com; 102 (1), David Fleetham - VWPics/Newscom; 102 (2), Chien Lee/Minden Pictures; 103 (3), Hollandluchtfoto/Getty Images; 103 (4), Daniel Janzen/Janzen.upenn.edu/Caters News Agency; 103 (5), Kjell Sandved/Alamy Stock Photo; 103 (6), Staffan Widstrand/SPL/Minden Pictures; 103 (7), Thomas Marent/ardea.com; 103 (8), Robert Sisson/National Geographic Creative; 104 (1), CB2/ZOB/Wenn/Newscom; 104 (2), Amy Hinkle/Caters News Agency; 104 (3), Haron Markicevic/Mercury Press/Caters News Agency; 105 (4), Vasily Bogoyavlensky/AFP/Getty Images; 105 (5), Michael Lynch/EyeEm/Getty; 105 (6), DuyDo/Getty Images; 105 (7), be happy!/Getty Images; 105 (8), Moises Castillo/AP Photo; 106 (1), Eurasia Press/Getty Images; 106 (2), Zumapress/Alamy Stock Photo; 107 (3), Art Media/Heritage-Images/The Image Works; 107 (4), Look and Learn/Bridgeman Images; 107 (5), akg-images/The Image Works; 107 (6), Rich Fury/Invision/AP Photo; 107 (7), Popperfoto/Getty Images; 107 (8), Koichi Kamoshida/Getty Images; 108 (1), Finnbarr Webster/Rex/Shutterstock; 108 (2), Innespace/Zumapress/Newscom; 109 (3), Lynn Palmer/Alamy Stock Photo; 109 (4), Yonhap News/YNA/Newscom; 109 (5), Aurora Photos/Alamy Stock Photo; 109 (6), Liysa/Getty Images; 109 (7), Marcel Mochet/AFP/Getty Images; 109 (8), Miami Herald/Getty Images

THE PUBLISHER WOULD LIKE TO THANK THE FOLLOWING PEOPLE FOR PUTTING SO MUCH HARD WORK AND CREATIVITY INTO THIS BOOK:

Jen Agresta, Becky Baines, Julide Dengel, Nicole Lazarus, Lori Epstein, Danny Meldung, Kate Olesin, Sally Abbey, Molly Reid, Sarah Wassner Flynn, Brittany Moya Del Pino, and Jennifer Geddes.

Since 1888, the National Geographic Society has funded more than 12,000 research, exploration, and preservation projects around the world. The Society receives funds from National Geographic Partners, LLC, funded in part by your purchase. A portion of the proceeds from this book supports this vital work.

NATIONAL GEOGRAPHIC and Yellow Border Design are trademarks of the National Geographic Society, used under license.

For more information, visit natgeo.com/info, call 1-800-647-5463, or write to the following address:

National Geographic Partners
1145 17th Street N.W.
Washington, D.C. 20036-4688 U.S.A.

Visit us online at nationalgeographic.com/books

For librarians and teachers: ngchildrensbooks.org

More for kids from National Geographic:
kids.nationalgeographic.com

For information about special discounts for bulk purchases, please contact National Geographic Books Special Sales: specialsales@natgeo.com

For rights or permissions inquiries, please contact National Geographic Books Subsidiary Rights: bookrights@natgeo.com

Julide Dengel, *Art Director*
Nicole Lazarus, *Designer*

Paperback ISBN: 978-1-4263-2738-4
Reinforced library binding ISBN: 978-1-4263-2739-1

Printed in China
16/RRDS/1